WOMEN OF *Country Music*

Project Manager: Carol Cuellar
Cover Design: Joseph Klucar

BLUE

Words and Music by
BILL MACK

Blue - 3 - 1

B7
E7
lone-some for you.
Tears fill my eyes till I can't
A
D
A
Verse:
C♯7
see.
1. Three o-clock in the morn-
2. See additional lyrics
F♯7
ing,
here am I,
B7
E7
sit-tin' here so lone-ly,
so lone-some I could cry.

Verse 2:
Now that it's over, I realize
Those sweet words you whispered
Were nothing but lies.
(To Chorus:)

From the Touchstone Motion Picture "CON AIR"

HOW DO I LIVE

Words and Music by
DIANE WARREN

F♯m7
G♯m7
C♯m7
Em7/A
ba - by, you would take a - way ev - 'ry - thing
good in my life.
And tell me
𝄋 Chorus:
D
A
G
F♯m7
D
A
now, how do I live with - out you? I want to know.
How do I breathe with - out
G
F♯m7
Bm7
Em7
F♯m7
G(9)
you, if you ev - er go?
How do I ev - er,
ev - er sur - vive?
To Coda
1.
Em7/A
D
F♯m7/B
How do I,
how do I, oh, how do I
live?
2. With - out you,
2.
Em7/A
D
F♯m
Em7
how do I, oh, how do I
live?

Bm7
F♯m7
F♯m7/B
If
G♯m7
C♯m7
F♯m7
you ev - er leave,
ba - by, you would take a - way ev - 'ry - thing.
G♯m7
C♯m7
F♯m7
Need you with me.
Ba - by, 'coz you know that you're ev - 'ry - thing
G♯m7
C♯m7
Em7/A
D.S.𝄋 al Coda
good in my life.
And tell me

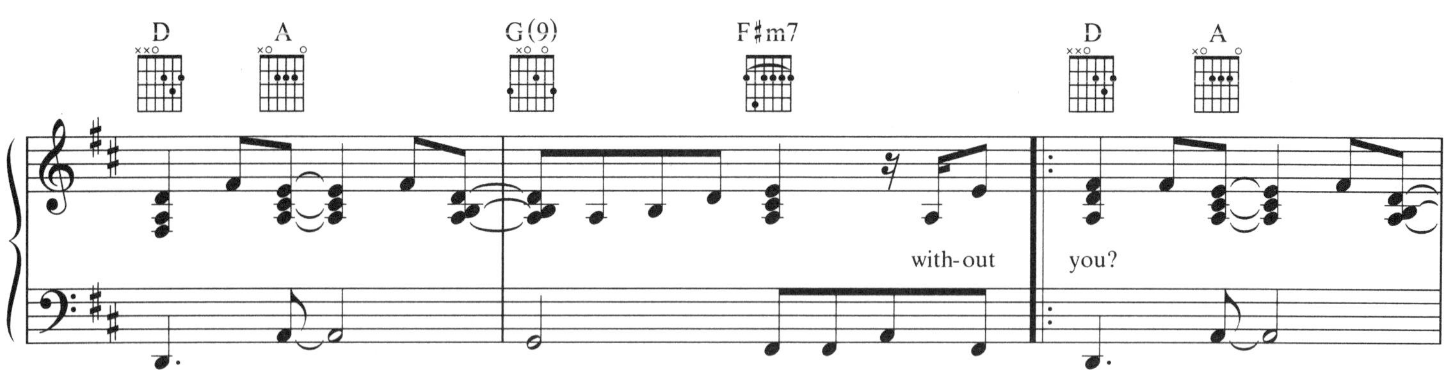

Repeat ad lib. and fade (vocal 1st time only)

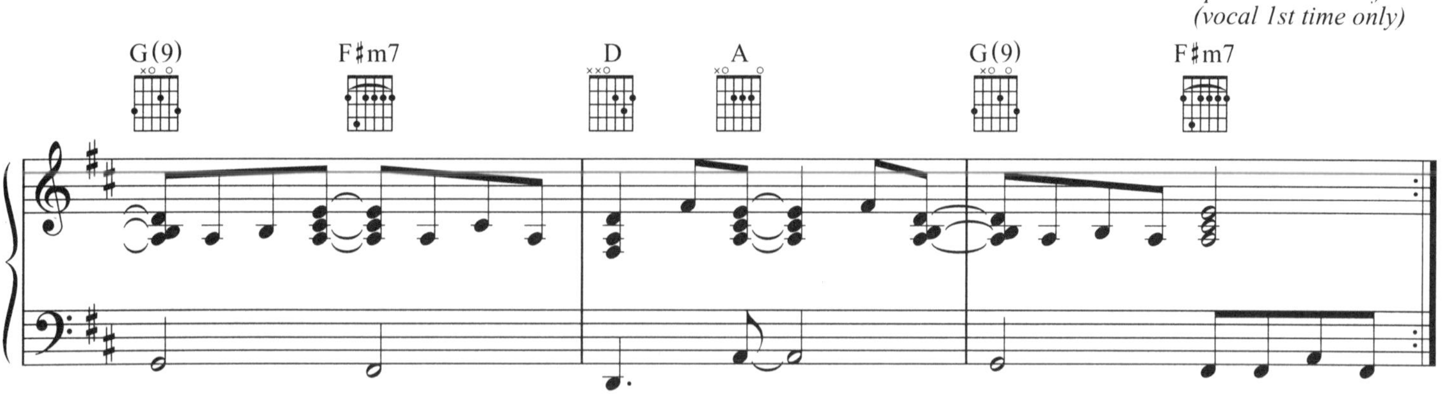

Verse 2:
Without you, there'd be no sun in my sky,
There would be no love in my life,
There'd be no world left for me.
And I, baby, I don't know what I would do,
I'd be lost if I lost you.
If you ever leave,
Baby, you would take away everything real in my life.
And tell me now...
(To Chorus:)

ALL THE GOOD ONES ARE GONE

Words and Music by
DEAN DILLON and BOB McDILL

Verse 2:
She's got friends down at the office,
And she can't help but notice
That when the day is over,
How they all hurry home.
Every day there's guys she works with,
And even some she flirts with,
But it seems like all the good ones are gone.
(To Chorus:)

Verse 3:
Once she had someone who loved her,
Back when she was younger.
And she wonders if she held out
A little bit too long.
Back then there were so many,
But now there just aren't any.
It seems like all the good ones are gone.
(To Chorus:)

ANY MAN OF MINE

still bet-ter love me. And
I can be late for a
date, that's fine, but he
bet-ter be on time.
2. And
Verse:
A♭5
N.C.
an-y man of mine-'ll say it
an-y man of mine bet-ter
A♭5
N.C.
fits just right when
dis-a-gree when I
E♭5
N.C.
last year's dress is just a
say an-oth-er wom-an's look-in'
A♭5
N.C.
lit-tle too tight. And an-y-
bet-ter than me. And
A♭5
N.C.
thing I do or say bet-ter
when I cook him din-ner and I
A♭5
N.C.
be o-kay when I
burn it black, he
E♭5
N.C.
have a bad hair day.
bet-ter say, "Mmmm, I
A♭5
N.C.
like it like that." Yeah!
Bridge:
C5
D♭5
N.C.
And if I
change my mind

G5
Ab5
N.C.
a mil - lion times,
C5
Db5
N.C.
I wan-na
hear him say,
Eb5
N.C.
"Yeah, yeah,
Eb5
N.C.
yeah, yeah,
Eb5
N.C.
yeah, I like it that
Eb5
N.C.
way!"
An - y man of
Country two-beat
Chorus:
Db
mine
bet-ter walk the
Ab
line.
Bet-ter show me a
Eb
teas - in', squeez - in',
pleas - in' kind of
Ab
time.
I need a man who

D♭
A♭
knows
how the sto - ry
goes.
He's got-ta be a
G♭
D♭
E♭
heart - beat-in', fine treat-in',
breath - tak-in', earth - quak-in'
kind,
1.
N.C.
A♭5
N.C.
A♭5
N.C.
an-y man of
mine.
E♭5
N.C.
A♭5
N.C.
2.
N.C.
an-y man of

D♭
A♭
mine.
(Instrumental solo...
D♭
E♭
Let me hear you say,
... end solo)
"Yeah, yeah,
yeah, yeah,
E♭7
N.C.
yeah, I like it that
way!"
An-y man, an-y
man, an-y man...
Chorus:
B♭
N.C.
E♭
B♭
An-y man of
mine
bet-ter walk the
line.
F
B♭
Bet-ter show me a
teas-in', squeez-in',
pleas-in' kind of
time.

Tag:
You gotta shimmy shake, make the earth quake.
Kick, turn, stomp, stomp, then you jump heel to toe, Do Si Do
'Til your boots wanna break, 'til your feet and your back ache
Keep it movin' 'til you just can't take anymore.
Come on, everybody on the floor, a-one two, a-three four.
Hup two, hup if you wanna be a man of mine, that's right.
This is what a woman wants...

CRY ON THE SHOULDER OF THE ROAD

Words and Music by
MATRACA BERG and TIM KREKEL

Cry on the Shoulder of the Road - 3 - 1

𝄋 Chorus:
E
A
D
A
ain't no tell - ing what I'll find, but I might as well move down the line, for
D
A
E
there's no com - fort here in your ZIP code. I'd rath - er
F♯m7
E/G♯
A
To Coda
Bm7
A/C♯
D
A
break - down on the high - way with no one to share my load,
D
E
1.
A
D/A
A
Bm7/A
and cry on the shoul - der of the road.
2.
A
E/G♯

Verse 2:
It makes me feel a little low,
Steel guitar on the radio,
And it's kinda scary the way these truckers fly.
So this is how leaving feels,
Drinking coffee and making deals
With the One above to get me through the night.
(To Chorus:)

DOES HE LOVE YOU

Words and Music by
BILLY STRITCH and SANDY KNOX

A
A+5
A6
one he rush-es home to, you're the one he gave his
(See additional lyrics)
Em7
A7
Dmaj 7
G9
name to. I nev-er see his face in the ear - ly morn-ing light. You have his
A/E
F♯m7
Bm7
Esus4
E7
A
morn - ings, his day - times and some-times I have his nights.
Em7
A7
D
D+5
But does he love you (does he love you) like he loves me? (like he loves me) Does he
f

D6
Am7
D7
Gmaj7
think of you (does he think of you) when he's hold - ing me? And does he whis - per all his
C9
D
Bm7
Em7
A7
fan - ta - sies? Does he love you (does he love you) like he's been lov - ing me?
1.
D
E/F♯
F♯m7
D
mp
Esus4
E
But when he's
2.
Gmaj7
C9

D
Bm7
Em7
A7
D
Oh,
G
D/F#
G/B
D/A
G
D/F#
should-n't I lose my tem - per, oh, and should-n't I be a - shamed? 'Cause I have ev'ry-thing to lose. And
Bm7/E
E7
G/A
3fr.
A7
A/B
B7
I, I have noth - ing to gain.
Oh, does he
E
E+5
love you (does he love you) like he loves me? (like he loves me) Does he

Additional Lyrics

2. But when he's with me, he says he needs me
And that he wants me, that he believes in me.
And when I'm in his arms, oh, he swears there's no one else.
Is he deceiving me or am I deceiving myself?
(To Chorus)

DADDY'S LITTLE GIRL

Words and Music by
ANGELA KASET, KENYA SLAUGHTER and STAN WEBB

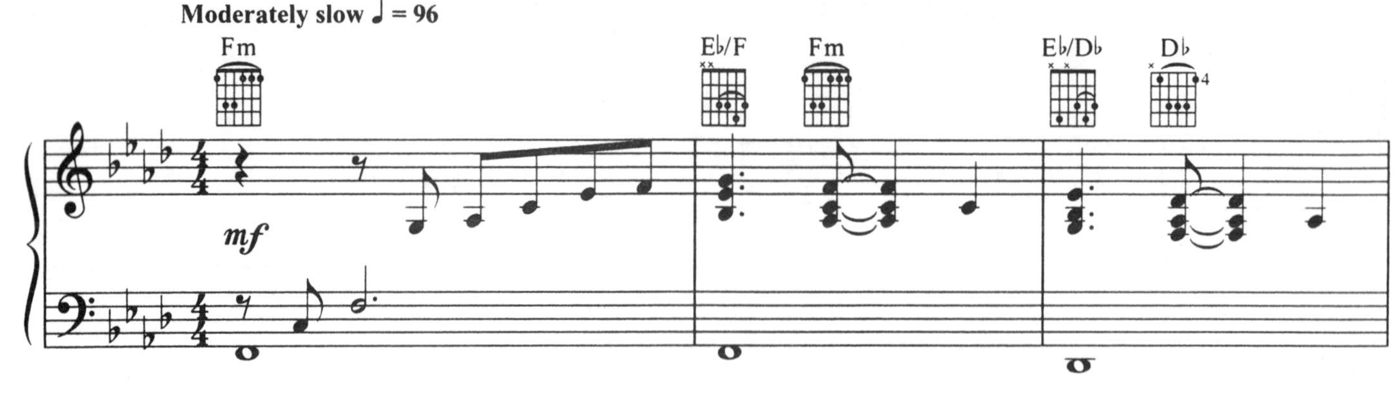
Moderately slow ♩ = 96
Fm
E♭/F
Fm
E♭/D♭
D♭
mf

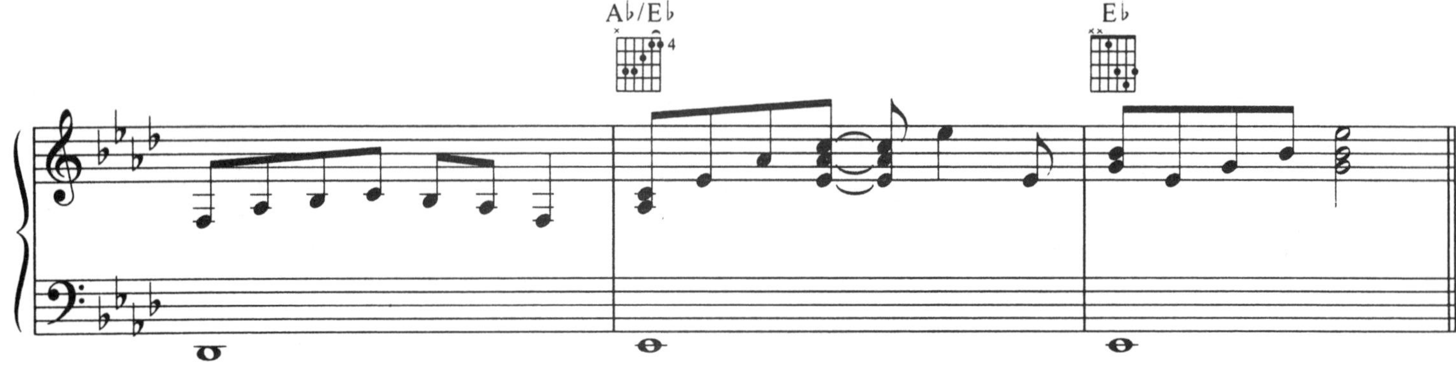
A♭/E♭
E♭

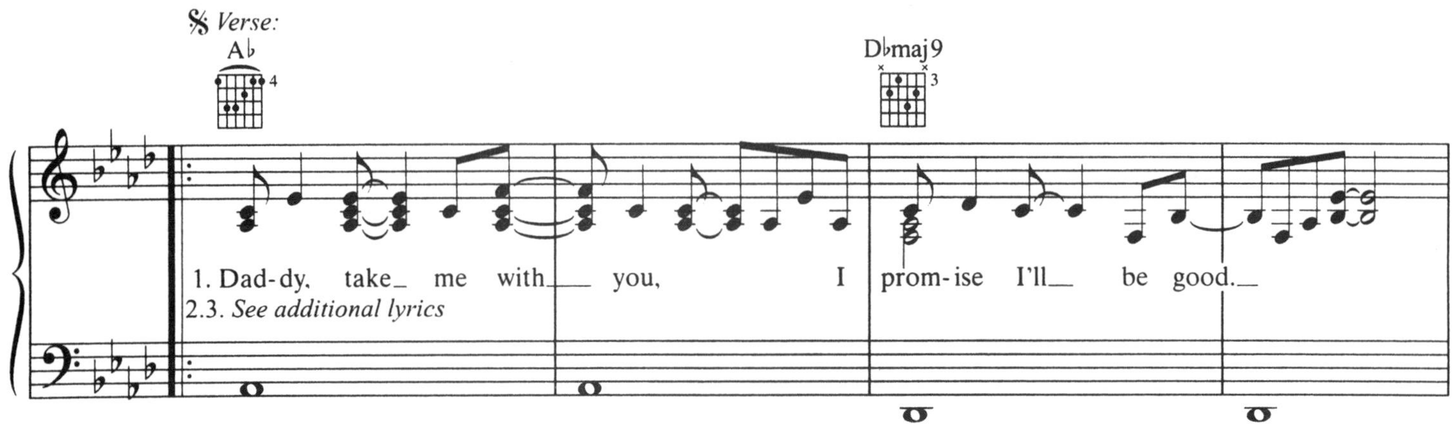
Verse:
A♭
D♭maj9
1. Dad-dy, take_ me with__ you, I prom-ise I'll_ be good._
2.3. See additional lyrics

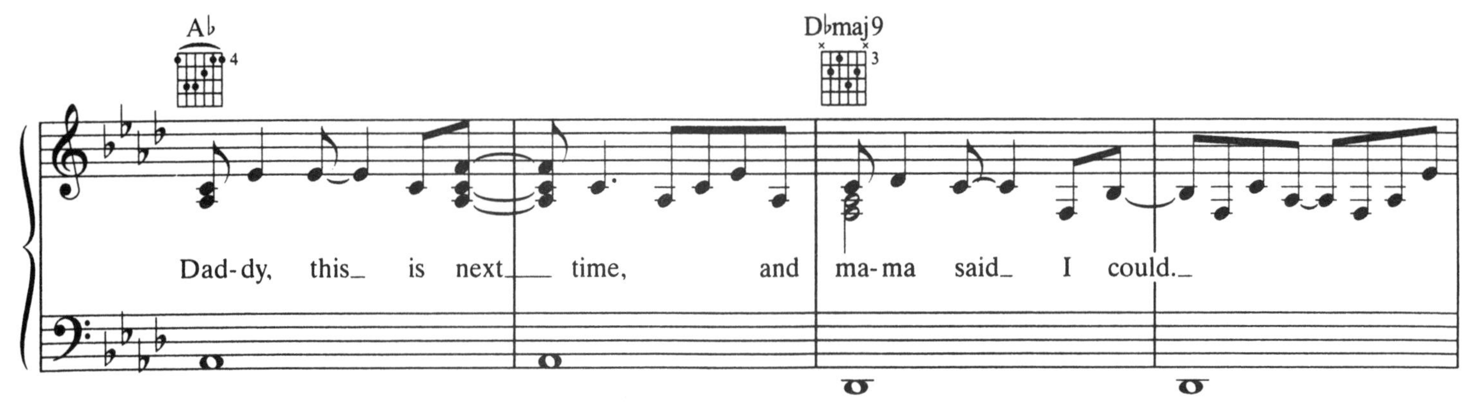
A♭
D♭maj9
Dad-dy, this_ is next__ time, and ma-ma said_ I could._

E♭
A♭
E♭
To Coda
Sit - tin' on the front seat, rid - in' down - town. For an ice - cream cone, I'd
D♭maj9
wrap him a - round my lit - tle fin - ger,
A♭
D♭maj9
A♭
tight-er than my ba - by curls. You can make a tear go a
D♭/A♭
A♭
E♭
1.
A♭
long, long way when you're Dad - dy's lit - tle girl.
Fm
E♭/F
Fm
E♭/D♭
D♭
A♭/E♭
E♭

2.
Bridge:
A♭
E♭/G
Fm
girl.
Well, he
tight-ened my bike chain from sev -
D♭
A♭
en to thir - teen,
taught me to drive when I
was a wild thing.
D♭
B♭7
Preached and he prayed when I made some mis - takes that I would - n't have made if I had
E♭
D.S.𝄋 al Coda
done it his way.
3. Now he
Coda
D♭maj9
say - in' to me...
Let me help you

A♭ D♭maj9

all I can___ while I'm still in___ this world.___

A♭ D♭/A♭ A♭

What-'ll you do___ when your Dad - dy's gone,___ and you're

E♭ A♭ E♭/F Fm

Dad - dy's___ lit - tle girl?

E♭/D♭ D♭ Fm D♭/A♭ A♭

rit.

What-'ll I do___ when my Dad - dy's___ gone?_

Verse 2:
Walkin' down the aisle with my eyes on Mr. Right,
My bouquet was shakin', Daddy held on tight.
Takin' those last steps, Daddy and me,
From the child to the woman I'd be.
With a diamond on my finger and my Mama's string of pearls,
He gave me away, 'cause I couldn't stay
Daddy's little girl.

Verse 3:
Now he hugs me when he sees me,
And we talk about the past.
He tries to give me money,
And I try to give it back.
He's a book of advice, more than I need.
The look in his eyes is sayin' to me...
Let me help you all I can
While I'm still in this world.
What'll you do when your Daddy's gone,
And you're Daddy's little girl?
What'll I do when my Daddy's gone?

A DOZEN RED ROSES

Words and Music by
JOHN GREENEBAUM, ARCHIE JORDAN
and CARRIE FOLKS

*Vocal sung one octave lower.

G♯m7
D♯m7
E
D♯m7
D♯
brides-maids gath-ered 'round her, the last de-tail's done. But a
All her friends wait-ed, the mu-sic soft-ly played, yet she
1.
G♯m7
D♯m7
E
F♯
B
doz-en red ros-es, who could they be from?
D♯m7
E
F♯
2. The
2.
G♯m7
reached for the
D♯m7
E
F♯
B
ros-es on the ta-ble where they lay.
Bridge:
E
D♯7
Then from the ros-es, she picked up an en-ve-lope.

G♯m7
D♯m/F♯
E
Her hand was guid - ed by__ her heart. And for
A♯m7(♭5)
D♯7
G♯m
G♯m/F♯
ev - er - y rose,_ a sin - gle tear - drop fell__ as she
E
F♯
lift - ed her veil__ and slow - ly read the card.
Verse:
C
Em7
F
F/G
G7
C
(Spoken:) "You're in your room sleeping as I write these words. I know you won't read them
Em7
F
G7
Am
Em
till years from now. (Sung:) God will call__ me home soon, I'll

F Em E7 Am Em
miss your wed-ding day, so your mom will keep_ this note to send_
F G7 C Am Em
with a rose bou-quet. So, take one of_ these ros - es_ to
F Em E7 Am Em
hold in your hand_ and I will be_ be - side_ you_ as
F F/G G7 N.C. C Em7
al - ways. rit. Love, (Spoken:) Dad." a tempo
F C F F/G G7 C
rit.

THE FOOL

Words and Music by
MARLA CANNON, CHARLEY STEFL
and GENE ELLSWORTH

Moderate country rock ♩ = 80

C F/A C/G F(9) C G6 G7

mp

C

𝄋 *Verse:*

C(9) F C

1. You don't know_ me, but I know who you are.__
2.3. *See additional lyrics*

mp

Am F C C(9)

Mind if I sit down?__ Do I look fa-mil - iar? If I

r.h.

F C Am G

don't, well, I should._ I'm sure you've seen me a - round.__

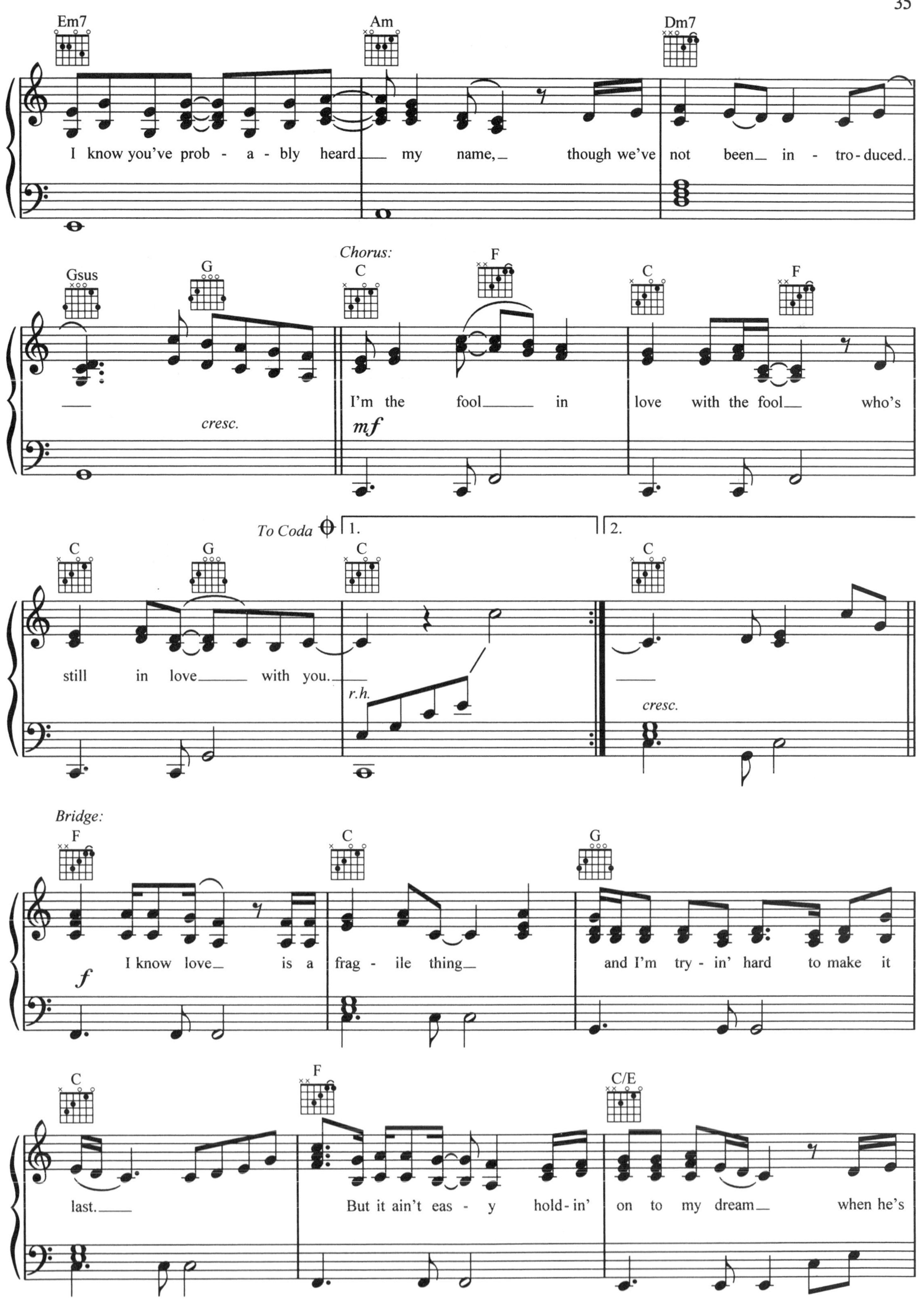

Em7
Am
Dm7
I know you've prob - a - bly heard my name, though we've not been in - tro - duced.
Gsus
G
Chorus:
C
F
C
F
cresc.
I'm the fool in love with the fool who's
mf
To Coda
1.
2.
C
G
C
C
still in love with you.
r.h.
cresc.
Bridge:
F
C
G
I know love is a frag - ile thing and I'm try - in' hard to make it
f
C
F
C/E
last. But it ain't eas - y hold - in' on to my dream when he's

Verse 2:
If you've got a minute, I'll buy you a drink,
I've got somethin' to say.
It might sound crazy, but last night in his sleep,
I heard him call out your name.
This ain't the first time, he's done it before,
And it's hard to face the truth.
(To Chorus:)

Verse 3:
Just one more thing before I go,
I'm not here to put you down.
You don't love him and that's a fact,
Girl, I've seen you around.
But you hold his heart in the palm of your hand
And it's breakin' mine in two.
(To Chorus:)

HURT ME

Words and Music by
DEBORAH ALLEN, RAFE VAN HOY
and BOBBY BRADDOCK

* Original recording in F♯ major.

G
D/E
Em
D/E
C
D7
G
D/E
Em
D/E
mf
hurt me.__ I still__ can't be-lieve__ you__ hurt me.__ And
hurt me.__ (Inst. solo ad lib....
C
D7
Bm
E7
Am7
just___ when I thought it___ was safe to___ come in, you__ let me want you__ and
D7
B7
C
C♯dim
need you,__ and__ then,_____ you left me__ like a child__ in the rain.__ Now I'm
...end solo) You left me__ like a child__ in the rain.__ Now I'm
cresc.
f
G/D
B/D♯
1.
Em
C
2.
Em
C
learn - ing my - self__ through the pain. Oh,__ you pain. Oh,__ you
lost____ in an o - cean of
dim.
dim.

G
D/E
Em
D/E
C
D7
hurt me.
mf
I fell in love, and it
G
D/E
Em
D/E
C
D7
Bm
E7
hurt me.
Can't you i-mag-ine how
I'm feel-ing now?
Am7
D
N.C.
2
Oh, will you ev-er know
how you
hurt me?
a tempo
mp
rit.
G
D/E
Em
D/E
C
D6
D7
G
rit. e dim.
p

A GIRL'S GOTTA DO
(What a Girl's Gotta Do)

Words and Music by
RICK BOWLES and ROBERT BYRNE

*Tune down 1/2 step.

Chorus:
G
C
F
C
Gb
B
E
B
town danc-ing till the break of dawn._ A girl's_ got-ta do what a
girl's got-ta do._ And now_ I got-ta get to get-ting o-ver you._ Too bad_
_ I got-ta do it with some-one new,_ but a girl's_ got-ta do what a
Am
G#m
1.
G/C
F#/B
girl's got-ta do._
2. Fan-
2.
girl's got-ta do._

F
C
G
C
F
C
G
E
B
G♭
B
E
B
G♭
F
C
G
Am
G
F
C
G
C
E
B
G♭
G♯m
G♭
E
B
G♭
B
Bridge:
Am
F
Dm7
C/E
F
G♯m
E
C♯m7
B/D♯
E
Give me a call some - time real soon and re - mind me to re - mem - ber to for - get a - bout
G
A
Chorus:
G
D
G♭
A♭
G♭
D♭
you, oh, yeah. A girl's got - ta do what a
A
D
G
D
A
A♭
D♭
G♭
D♭
A♭
girl's got - ta do. And now I got - ta get to get - ting o - ver you. Too bad

Verse 2:
Fancy meeting you at our stomping ground,
Sorry if you caught me painting the town.
Guess you should've stayed home with your memory,
Baby, don't take it personally.
(To Chorus:)

GO AWAY, NO WAIT A MINUTE

Words and Music by
CATHY MAJESKI, SUNNY RUSS
and STEPHONY SMITH

A
world.
Go a - way, no, wait a
𝄋 Chorus:
D
G
min- ute.
I want out, then I want in it.
A
I'm all con-fused, but I ad - mit it.
Go a - way, no, wait a
D
To Coda
1.
N.C.
2.
min- ute.
2. C'est la vie, la vie.
G
D

A
D
I need
Bridge:
G7
D
some help, I'm not quite my-self. And late-ly, I'm a ner-vous wreck.
G7
My whole world has changed, the rea-son I'm strange is I
E
A7(♯5)
D.S. 𝄋 al Coda
love you and, ba-by, that scares me to death. Go a-way, no, wait a

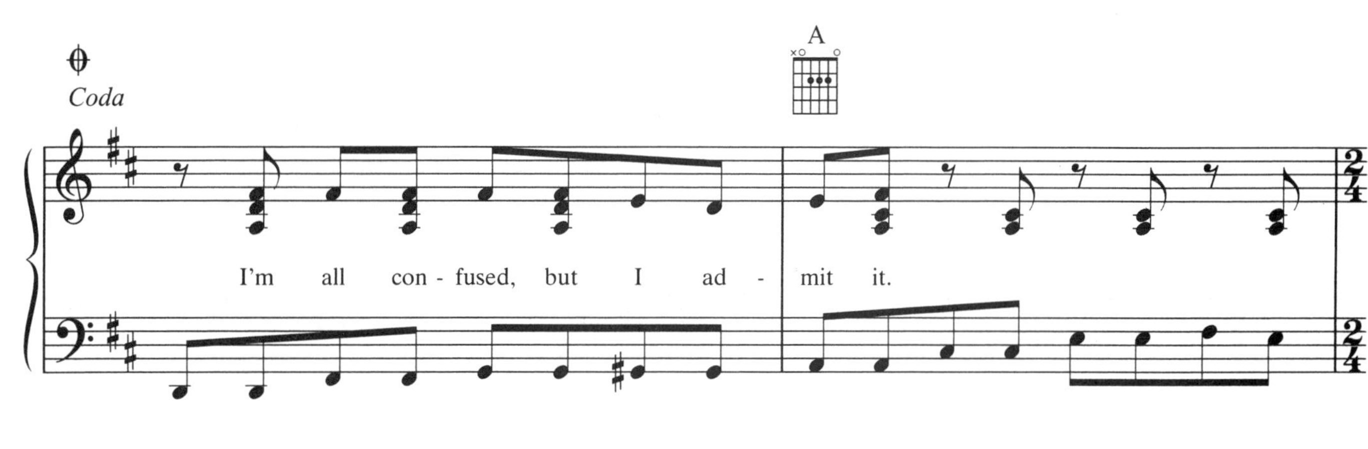

Verse 2:
C'est la vie, la vie,
That's what you get when you get me.
I have the right to change my mind
At least a couple hundred times.
(To Chorus:)

GOOD AS I WAS TO YOU

Words and Music by
BILLY LIVSEY and DON SCHLITZ

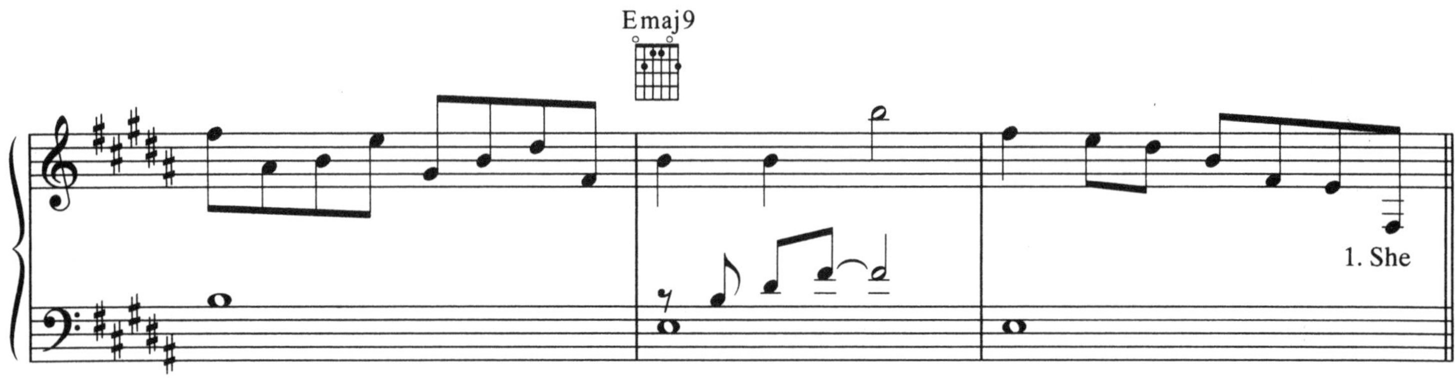

E
F♯
He was sit - ting at their ta - ble with
F♯7
B
some-one new_ this time.___ She walked up right be - side___ him, her
B/D♯
E
F♯
face did not___ turn red.___ She looked at him so calm -
F♯7
B
B/D♯
ly and this is what she said:___ "Good as I was to you,
𝄋 Chorus:
E
F♯7
___ is this the thanks_ I get?___ Are all the years_ we shared
3. (Inst. solo ad lib....

B
B/D♯
E
so eas - y to for - get?
...end solo)
1.3. Does
2. Is
C♯m7
this mean that you've won? Are you fi - n'lly hav - ing fun?
this the way it's done, look - ing out for num - ber one?
F♯
G♯m7
Is she your dream come true?
Did you think it through?
D♯m7
C♯m7
To Coda
Oh, she sure looks good, but she won't ev - er be
1.
F♯7sus
F♯7
B
good as I was to you."

Verse 2:
The room got awfully quiet,
Everybody stared.
Finally the waiter said,
"Should I bring another chair?"
She said, "No, I was just leaving,"
But as she walked out the door,
She said, "Honey, you can have him,
I don't want him anymore."
(To Chorus:)

GUYS DO IT ALL THE TIME

Words and Music by
ROBERT BRUCE WHITESIDE
and KIM TRIBBLE

Moderate country rock ♩ = 84
C
mf

Verse:
1. Got in this morn-in' at 4 A. M., you're as mad as you can be. I was
2. See additional lyrics

G
drink-in' and talk - in' and you know how that goes, time just slipped a - way from me. By the

time I knew what time it was, it was
too late to call home. Stop

G
car - ryin' on, act like a child, I
was - n't do - in' an - y - thing wrong.

Chorus:
C
F
C
Guys do it all the time, and you ex - pect us to un - der - stand. When the
f (Instrumental solo on D.S....

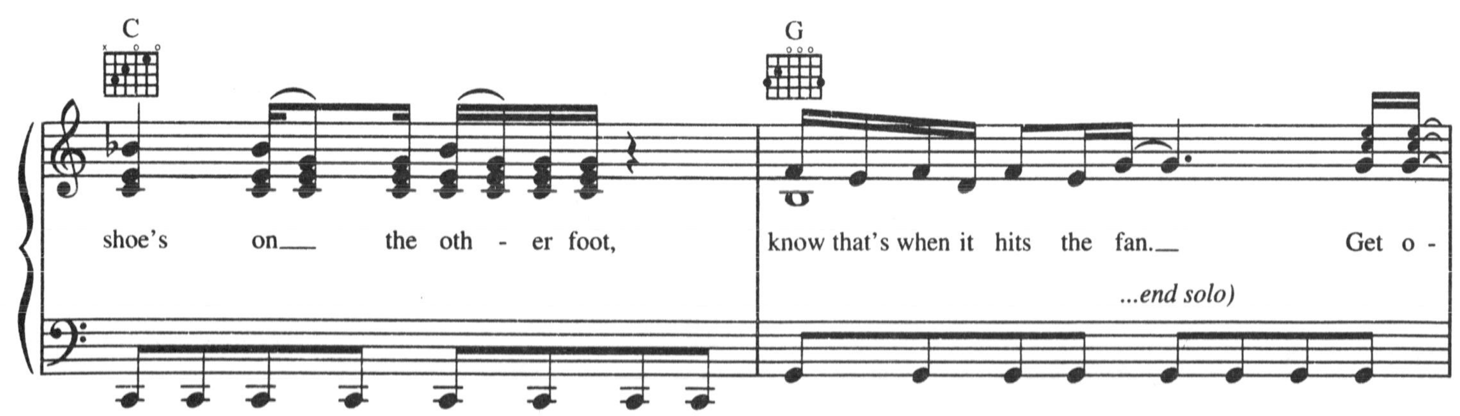
C
G
shoe's on the oth - er foot, know that's when it hits the fan. Get o -
...end solo)

C
- ver it hon - ey, that's a two - way street, or you
won't be a man of

F
N.C.
G
mine. Sure I
had some beers with the girls last night,

To Coda
B♭
G
N.C.
C
guys do it all the time.

1.
2.
2. I know I

Bridge:

F C

You look like__ you just took__ a long__ look in the mir - ror.

F G *D.S. 𝄋 al Coda*

Tell me, ba - by, if things don't look a whole lot clear - er.

𝄌 *Coda*

C

Repeat ad lib. and fade

Verse 2:
I know I left my clothes all over the place and I took your twenty bucks.
No, I didn't get the front yard cut 'cause I had to wash my truck.
Will you bring me a cold one, baby?
Turn on the TV.
We'll talk about this later,
There's a ball game I wanna see.
(To Chorus:)

HOW DO I GET THERE

Words and Music by
CHRIS FARREN and DEANA CARTER

D Em
F Gm

— see a dif - fer - ent light — a - round you. — One thing — I —

D/F♯ G D/F♯
F/A B♭ F/A

— have-n't told — you, — I just wan-na hold — you — and nev - er let go. —

Em Em7/A
Gm Gm7/C

— I need — to know: —

cresc.

Chorus:

D
F

How do I get there from here?

mf

G Em7 A7sus
B♭ Gm7 C7sus

How do I make you see? How do I tell you what my heart's been tell - in' me?

D G
F B♭

Lost in your lov - in' arms, that's where I wan - na be. — You know I love you. —

1.
Em7
Gm7
Em7/A
Gm7/C
D
F
D(9)
F(9)
How do I get there?
2.
Bridge:
G
B♭
The short-est dis - tance be-tween two points is a
D/F♯
F/A
straight line, but I'll climb an - y moun-tain that you want me to climb. The per-
Em
Gm
- fect com - bi - na - tion is your heart and mine. Dar - lin', won't you give me a sign?

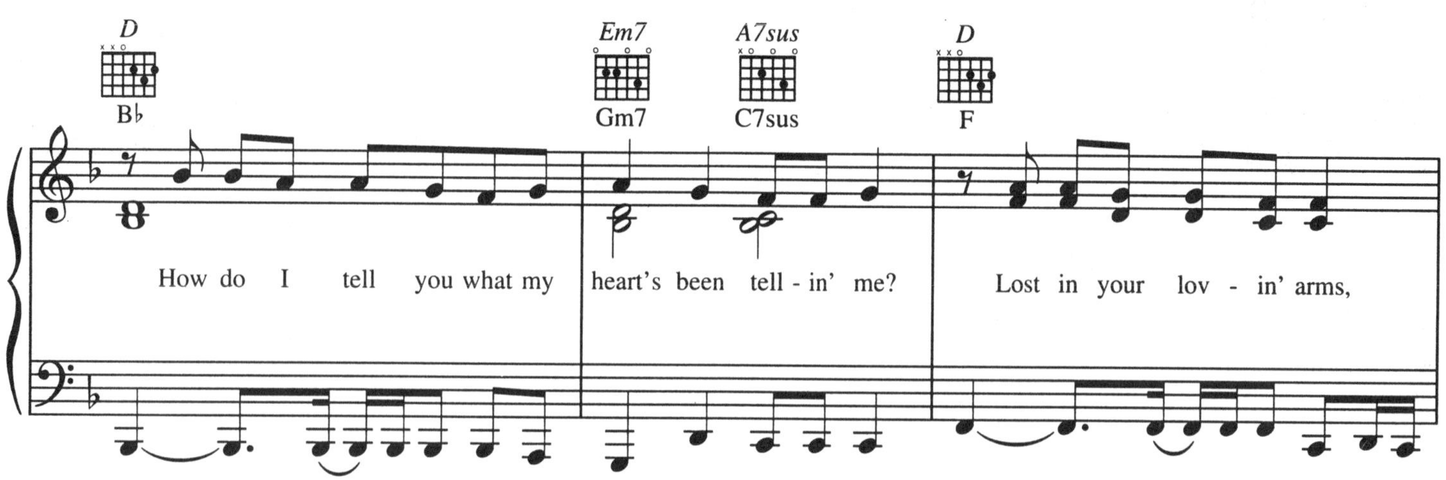

Verse 2:
You probably think I've lost my mind,
Takin' this chance, crossin' that line.
But I promise to be truer than true,
Dreamin' every night with these arms around you.
I can't wait any longer, this feeling's gettin' stronger;
Help me find a way.
(To Chorus:)

WHAT IF IT'S YOU

Words and Music by
CATHY MAJESKI and
ROBERT ELLIS ORRALL

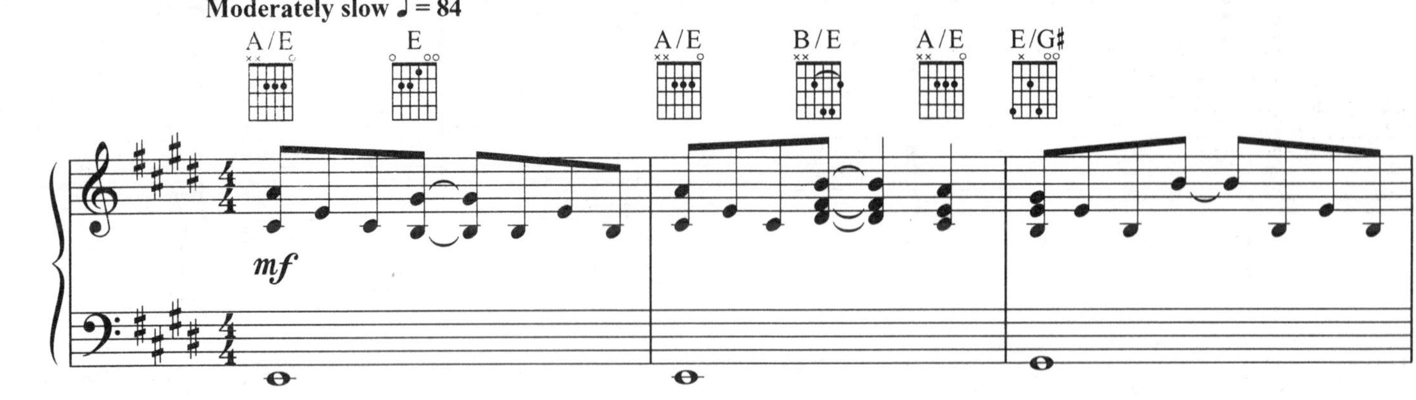

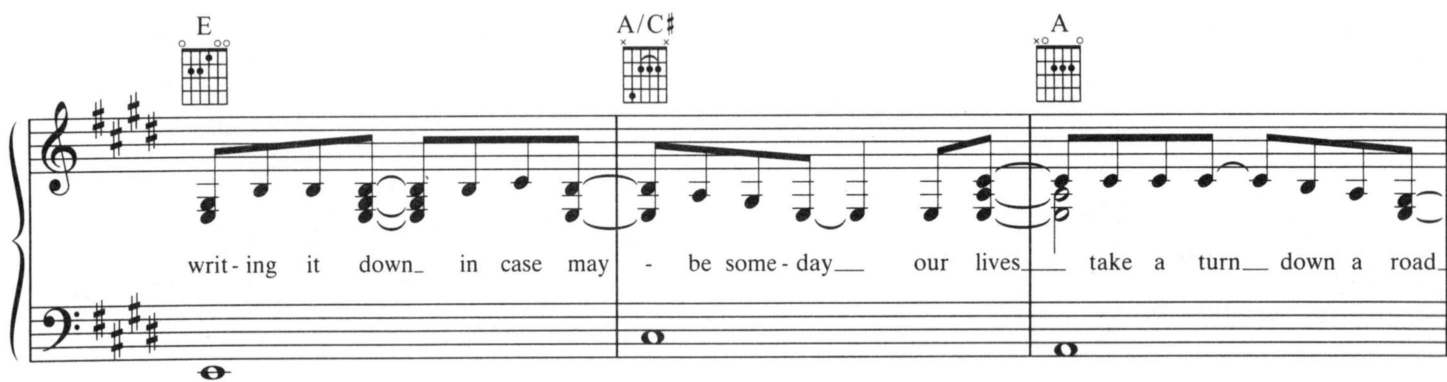

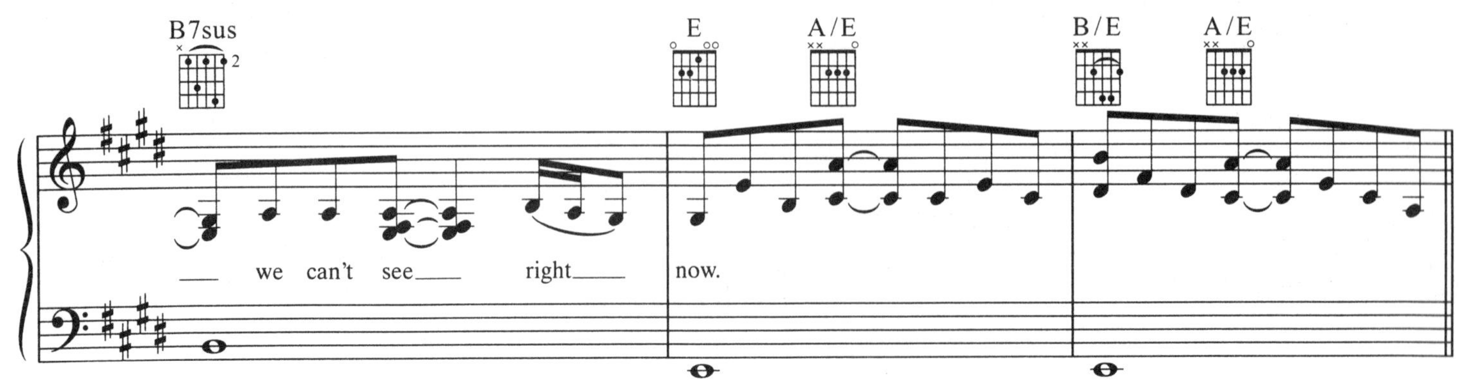

Verses 2 & 3:
E
A/C♯
E
2. I know you're hap - py, and I'm hap - py for you. But since you found each oth - er, I've been
3. See additional lyrics
A/C♯
A
B/A
A
B/A
so con - fused 'cause I be - lieve there's one soul on this earth that was meant for mine,
E
C♯m7
Chorus:
Amaj9
I was sent here to find. What if it's you?
Bsus
B
E
A/E
E
What if our hearts were meant to be one? What-'ll I do,
Amaj9
Bsus
B
E
B/D♯
know - ing that I'll nev - er love an - y - one as

C♯m7
E/B
F♯m7
1.
B7sus
much as I do love you? What if it's true? What if it's you?
A/E
E
A/E
B/E
A/E
E/G♯
2.
A
B7sus
B7sus
A/E
E
3. If
What if it's you?
Bridge:
A/E
E
E/G♯
A(9)
If I ev-er hold you, I'll nev-er let go. But if
E/G♯
A(9)
B7sus
B7
N.C.
I nev-er do, how will I know? What if it's you?

Verse 3:
If destiny called and I missed my cue,
Do I get one more chance?
Oh, how I wish I knew.
I'll never again put my heart in the hands of fate
If it's too late.
(To Chorus:)

I CAN'T DO THAT ANYMORE

Words and Music by
ALAN JACKSON

Dsus
D
G
C
D
think that I___ should stay.
I used to dream a-bout
what I would be.___

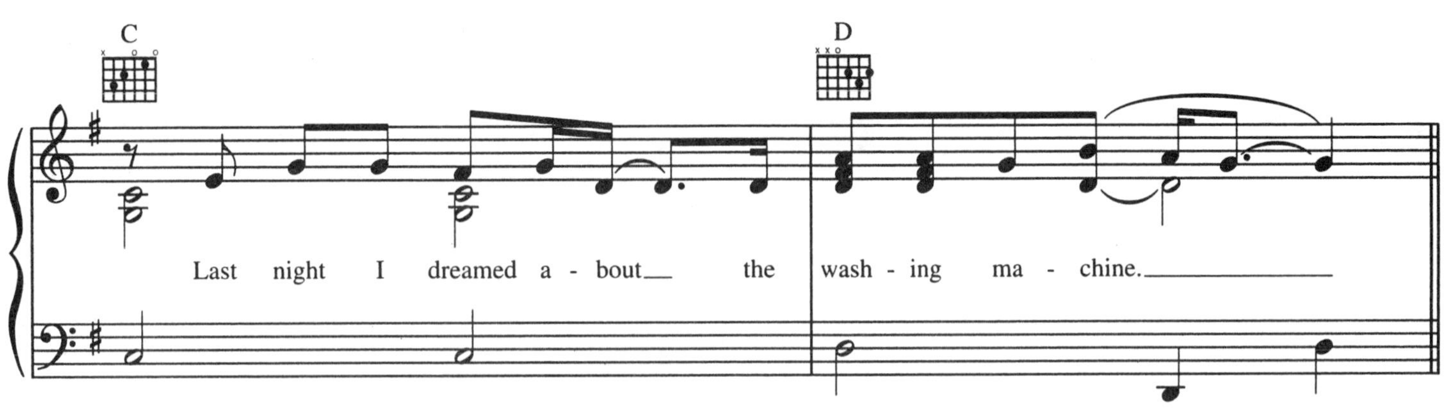
C
D
Last night I dreamed a - bout___ the
wash - ing ma - chine.___

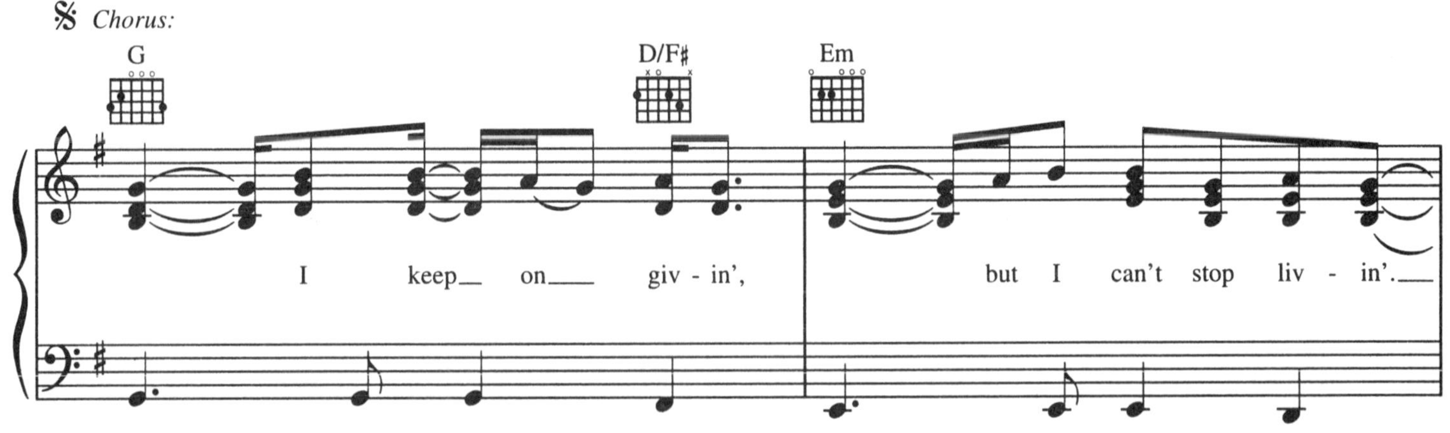
Chorus:
G
D/F♯
Em
I keep___ on___ giv - in',
but I can't stop liv - in'.___

C
Dsus
D
___ A wom-an needs___ a lit - tle
some-thing of her own.___

G
D/F♯
Em
C
To Coda
I like hap - py end - ings.
I don't like de - pend - ing.
I keep right on pre - tend - ing,

1.
D
G
Em
but I can't do that an - y - more.

C
G/D
D
2.
D
G
but I can't do that an - y - more.

Bridge:
Em
C
D
You try to tell me I'm not be - in' fair to you.

Verse 2:
Now, you say I'm bein' silly,
But you don't know me, really.
You never take the time to ask me how I feel.
I keep the checkbook balanced.
I decorate your palace.
You know that I used to think that you were king.
Somewhere deep down I know you really love me.
But you can't see that what we have was not all I needed.
(To Chorus:)

(If You're Not in It for Love) I'M OUTTA HERE!

Words and Music by
SHANIA TWAIN and
ROBERT JOHN "MUTT" LANGE

* Vocal sung one octave lower.

B♭5

It's the same old line,
He says, "Come be a star
Now, tell me, what's your sign?

F5

oh, ev - er - y time. Are you here a - lone?
in the back seat of my car." Oh, but ba - by, slow
Why al - ways the same old line? I'll be in num - ber four

C5 G5 C5

Can I take you home?
down, you're go - in' way too far.
oh nine if you change your mind.

1. 2.3. F7

2. Now, ev - 'ry wom - an sees Let me make it clear to you,

A♭ B♭5 N.C.

my dear. If you're not

Chorus:
Ab
Eb
Bb
in it for love,
if you're not will - in' to give
it all you've got, if you're not in it for life,
if you're not in it for love, let me make
To Coda
F5
Bb5
N.C.
it clear to you, my dear,

C5
if you're not in it for love,
I'm out - ta here.
D.S. 𝄋 al Coda
3. Babe, I can change your world,
Coda
B♭
A♭
B♭
if you're not in it for life,
if you're not
A♭
B♭
in it for love,
B♭5
C5
N.C.
B♭5
C5
I'm out - ta here.
molto rit.

IS THERE LIFE OUT THERE

Words and Music by
SUSAN LONGACRE and RICK GILES

Ab
Gb(addAb)
Ab
4fr.
Now she's feel - ing that there's some-thing more. Is there
Db
Db/Gb
Gb
Db
life out there? So much she has-n't done. Is there life be - yond her fam-
Bbm7
Ab
Db
Db/Gb
Gb
'ly and her home? She's done what she should, should she do what she dares? She
Bbm7
Ab
1.
Db
does-n't wan-na leave, she's just won-d'ring is there life out there?
Gb
Db
Gb
She's al -

2.
Db
4fr.
There's a
Ab
4fr.
Db
4fr.
place in the sun that she's nev - er been, where
Gb(addAb)
Ab
4fr.
life is fair and time is a frend. Would she
Ab/C
Db
4fr.
Gb
do it the same as she did back then? Oh, she
Gb(addAb)
Ab
4fr.
Bb
looks out her win - dow and she won - ders a - gain. Is there

Additional lyrics

2. She's always lived for tomorrow,
   She's never learned how to live for today.
   Oh, she's dying to try something foolish,
   Do something crazy or just get away.
   Oh, something for herself for a change.

   (To Chorus)

IT MATTERS TO ME

Words and Music by
ED HILL and MARK D. SANDERS

F♯
B
D♯m7
B(9)
then waltz back in - to my life
like it's all gon - na be al - right.
A♯m
C♯
Don't you know how much I
hurt?
When_ we don't
Chorus:
F♯
D♯m7
B(9)
C♯
talk, when we don't touch, when it does - n't
feel like we're ev - en in love,_
F♯
D♯m7
B(9)
C♯
it mat - ters to me._
When I don't_ know what to
F♯
D♯m7
B(9)
C♯
say, don't know what to do, don't know if it
real - ly ev - en mat - ters to you._

F♯
D♯m7
B(9)
C♯
How can I make you see, it mat - ters to me?
1.
2.
Oh, when I don't know what to
say, don't know what to do, don't know if it real - ly ev - en mat - ters to you.

F♯ D♯m7 B(9) C♯

How can I make you see, oh, it mat - ters to me?

F♯ D♯m7 B(9) C♯

It mat - ters to me.

F♯ D♯m7 B(9) C♯

It mat - ters to

F♯ D♯m7 B(9) C♯ G♯m7/C♯ F♯

me.

rit.

Verse 2:
Maybe I still don't understand
The distance between a woman and a man.
Tell me how far it is,
And how you can love like this.
I'm not sure I can.
(To Chorus:)

JUST THE SAME

Words and Music by
TOM SHAPIRO, CHRIS WATERS
and TERRI CLARK

A(9)
bench,
a Sun - day pa - per at your feet.
E
A/C♯
If you'd been wait - in' for a tax -
cresc.
D
E
i
3. See additional lyrics
mf
or at a bus stop in the
D
A
rain,
I would-'ve
C♯m
D
E
To Coda
found you,
I would-'ve
found you
just the same.

1.
A
E
2. You know you could_ have been_ a gam-
2.
A
E/G♯
No, it real - ly did - n't mat -
Bridge:
F♯m
D
ter, who you'd been_ or what_ you'd done._
A
D
A
E/G♯
Where we met or when it
F♯m
Bm
D/A
hap - pened,_ you'd_ still be_ the one._

Verse 2:
You know you could have been a gambler
Whose luck was runnin' low
Or just another drifter
Without a single place to go.
You could have been a broken dreamer
Without a penny to your name.
I would've loved you, I would have loved you
Just the same.
(To Bridge:)

Verse 3:
There's no way to know the future,
But one thing will never change.
I'm gonna love you, I'm gonna love you
Just the same.

LAND OF THE LIVING

Words and Music by
TIA SILLERS and WAYLAND PATTON

A E B C♯m A E

takes be-come clear - er___ af - ter the fact.______

B C♯m A E B C♯m

Now, when you pick up the piec - es, but you

A E C♯m B A E

can't make them fit, don't waste all your time try'n' to

B C♯m A E B

make sense of it.________

𝄋 *Chorus:*

A E B C♯m7 A E

Just hur - ry back to the land of the liv - ing. Things have changed since

B
A
E
B
C♯m7
you've been gone.
The world is turn-ing in the land of the liv - ing.
A
E
To Coda
1.
B
E
A(9)
Take a deep breath, life goes on.
C♯m7
B
A(9)
E
B
C♯m7
Life goes on.
2. Come
2.
B
A(9)
E
B
C♯m7
life goes on.
Life goes on.
A(9)
E
B
A(9)
E
(Inst. solo ad lib....

B C♯m7 A(9) E B

...end solo)

Bridge:

Lean on my shoul - der and

A E A(9) E/G♯

whis - per your tears. We all need some - one to

A(9) B N.C. *D.S.* 𝄋 *al Coda*

ech - o our fears. Oh.

𝄌 *Coda*

B A(9) E B C♯m7

life goes on. Life goes on

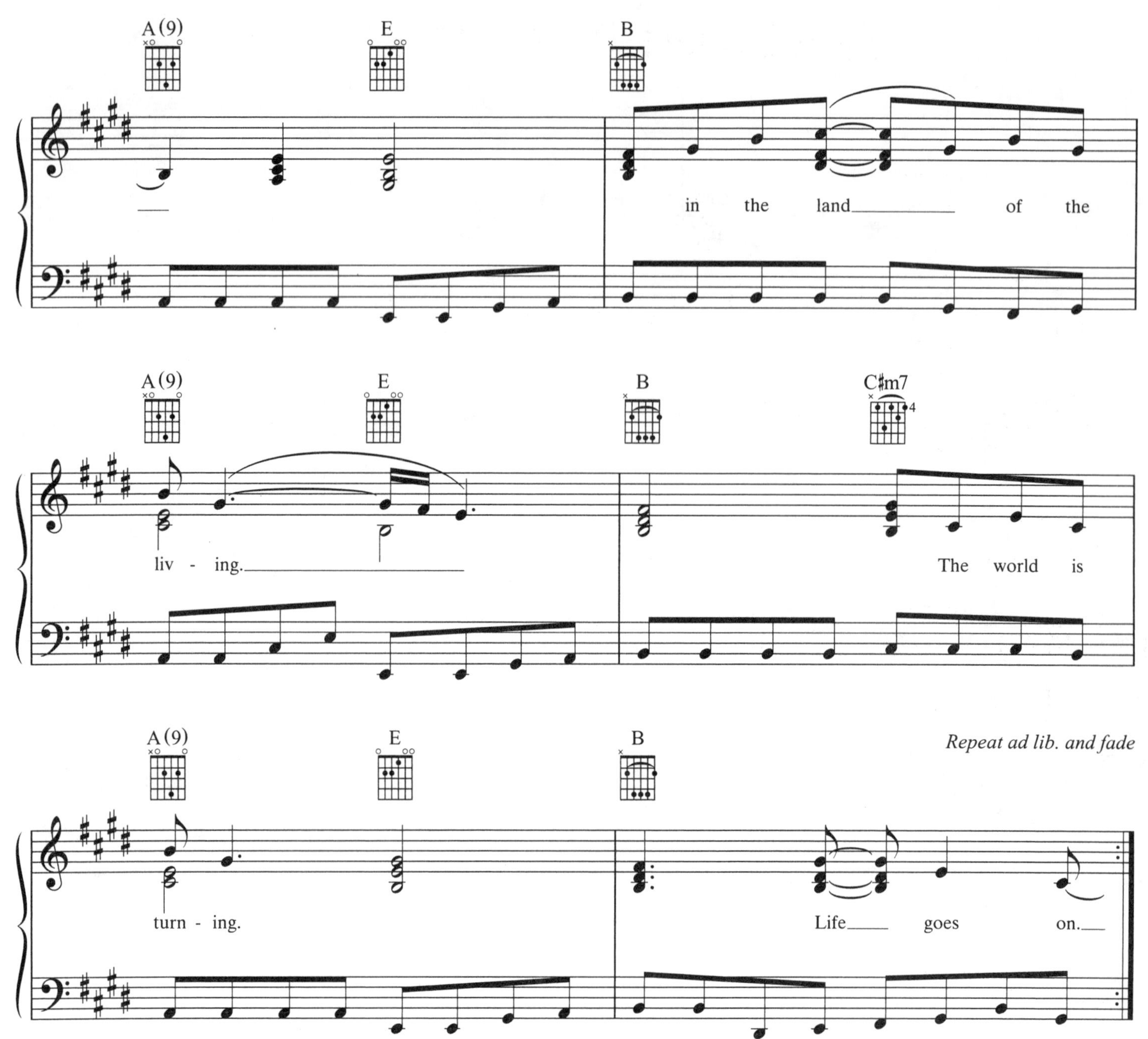

Verse 2:
Come down from that dark cloud,
What's done is done.
Don't you go down believing
You're the only one
That ever felt heartache turn to regret.
We've all got something we'd like to forget.
(To Chorus:)

THE LIGHT IN YOUR EYES

Words and Music by
DAN TYLER

D
Bm7
A
G2
don't ev - er lose the light in your eyes,
don't ev - er lose the
1.3.
2.4.
D2
light in your eyes.
cresc.
Bridge:
Bm
G
Keep on shin - ing,
keep on smil - ing.
don't lose faith and
f
don't lose heart.
When you're cry - ing,
just keep try - ing to re -
mind your - self, you're a shin - ing star,
1.
D.S.
yes, you are.
dim.

Verse 2:
People make you promises they'll never keep;
Soon you'll know why people say, "Talk is cheap."
Life resembles one big compromise,
But don't ever lose the light in your eyes,
Don't ever lose the light in your eyes.
(To Bridge:)

Verse 3: Instrumental solo ad lib.

Verse 4:
Somewhere down the line, you'll face the judgment day;
When the angels look at you, what will you say?
They've got a way of knowing who qualifies;
Just let 'em see the light in your eyes,
Don't ever lose the light in your eyes.
(To Bridge:)

NEVER AGAIN, AGAIN

Words and Music by
MONTY HOLMES
and BARBIE ISHAM

B
F♯
F♯7
I'll say nev-er a-gain, a-gain. Each
Verse:
B
C♯7
F♯
time you leave, I say I've had e-nough. But I
B
C♯7
F♯
must be ad-dict-ed to your kind of love. I
A♯7
B
A♯7
A7
swear to my-self I'm gon-na stand my ground. But one
G♯7
C♯7
look at you breaks my de-fens-es down. And here comes nev-er a-

Chorus:
F♯
G7
G♯7
gain, a-gain.
Once more I'll let you back in.
Then just like it's
C♯7
B
F♯
To Coda
al - ways been,
I'll say nev-er a-gain, a-gain.
D.S. al Coda
B
C♯7
F♯
G♯m
A7
I
Coda
C♯7/E♯
D♯m7
C♯7
Then just like it's al - ways been,
I'll say
B
F♯
C♯7
F♯
nev - er a - gain, a - gain.

ONE WAY TICKET
(Because I Can)

Words and Music by
JUDY RODMAN and KEITH HINTON

A Bm7 A/C♯ D

There's a new ho - ri - zon, and the

G D A Em7 D/F♯

prom - ise of a fa - vor - able wind. I'm head - ing out to - night, trav -

G Bm7 A N.C.

- el - ing light; I'm gon - na start all o - ver a - gain... And buy a

cresc.

Chorus:

D Bm7 A

one way tick - et on a west - bound train to see how far I can go.

G D Bm7

Gon - na go out danc - ing in the pour - ing rain,

(Be - cause I can.)

A
G
Bm
A
talk to some-one I don't_ know.___
I will
face the world_______ a-round_
(Be-cause I can.____)
Em7
D/F♯
G
D/F♯
___ me, know-ing that I'm
strong e-nough to let you__ go;____
and I will
G
Bm
A
1. D
Bm7
fall in love______ a-gain,___
be-cause I can.____
A
G2
D/F♯
2. D
I have
Bridge:
C2
Em7
D
C2
G
D
walked through the fire, and
crawled on my knees_ through the
val-ley of the shad-ow of doubt;_
f

C2
Em
G
D
and the truth came shin-ing like a light on me, and
A
N.C.
Chorus:
E
now I can see my way out. I'm gon-na buy a one way tick-et on a
cresc.
ff
C♯m7
B
A2
west-bound train to see how far I can go. Gon-na
(Be-cause I can.
E
C♯m7
B
go out danc-ing in the pour-ing rain, and talk to some-one I don't know.
)
A2
E
C♯m7
I'm gon-na buy a one way tick-et on a west-bound train, gon-na

Verse 2:
I'm gonna climb that mountain
And look the eagle in the eye.
I won't let them clip my wings
And tell me how high I can fly.
How could I have ever believed
That love had to be so blind
When freedom was waiting down at the station?
All I had to do was make up my mind...
(To Chorus:)

POOR, POOR PITIFUL ME

Words and Music by
WARREN ZEVON

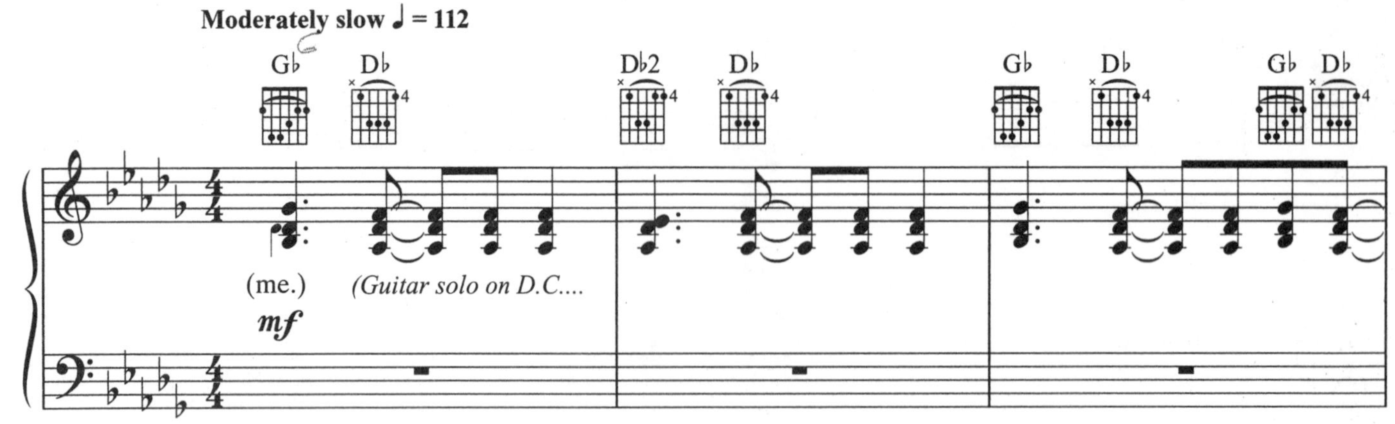

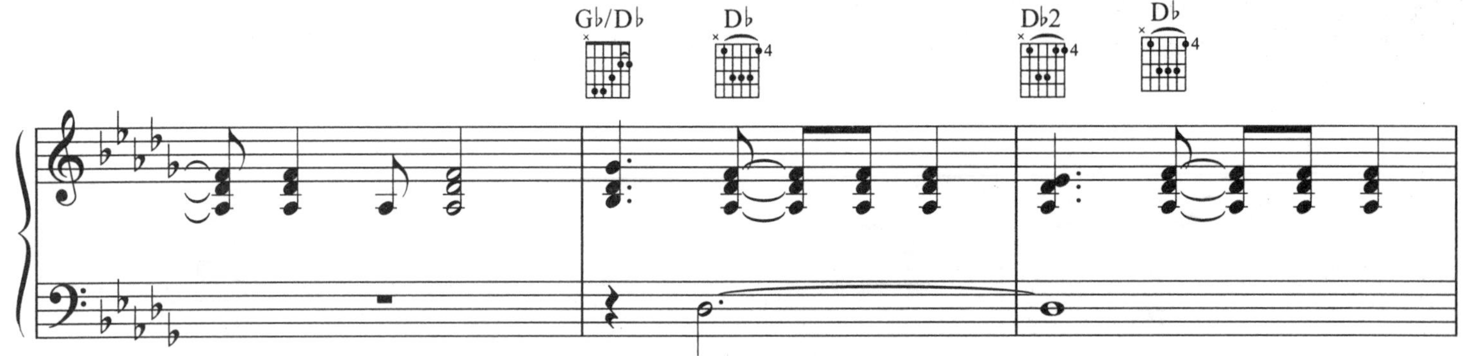

train don't run through here no more.
Poor, poor pit-i-ful me.
Chorus:
Gb G
Db D
Ab5 A
Db D
Poor, poor pit-i-ful me!
Gb G
Db D
Poor, poor pit-i-ful me!
Gb G
Db D
Oh, these boys won't let me be.
Ab5 A
Db D
Gb G
Ab5 A
Lord, have mer-cy on me.
To Coda
Gb/Db G
Db
Db2
Db
Woe, woe is me.

Gb/Db
Db
Gb/Db
Db
Verse:
Db5
2. Well, I met a man out in Hol-ly-wood, and I ain't nam-in' names. But he real-ly worked me o-ver good, just like Jes-se James.
Gb
Db5
Yes, he real-ly worked me o-ver good, he was a cred-it to his gen-der. He put me through some
Gb
Db5

chang-es, Lord, sort - a like a War-ing blend-er.
Chorus:
G♭ D♭ A♭5 D♭ G♭ D♭
Poor, poor pit - i - ful me! Poor, poor pit - i - ful me!
G♭ D♭ A♭5 D♭
Oh, these boys won't let me be.
G♭ A♭5
D.C. al Coda
Lord, have mer - cy on me. Woe, woe is
Coda
G♭ D♭ D♭2 D♭ G♭ D♭ G♭ D♭
me.

Verse 3:
Well, I met a boy in the Vieux-Carres,
Down in Yokohama.
He picked me up and he threw me down,
Sayin', "Please don't hurt me, mama."
(To Chorus:)

TWO SPARROWS IN A HURRICANE

Words and Music by
MARK ALAN SPRINGER

*Sing melody one octave lower.
**Play chord in parentheses 2nd time only.

D
E♭
B7
C7
B7sus
C7sus
B7
C7
they'll spread their wings___ and fly.___
Chorus:
Bm7
Cm7
E7
F7
A
B♭
D
E♭
Like two spar - rows in a hur - ri - cane,___
cresc.
mf
A
B♭
D
E♭
Bm7
Cm7
try - in' to find___ their way,___ with a head full of dreams,_ and
A/C♯ (Type 2)
B♭/D
E
F
A
B♭
faith that can move_ an - y - thing.___ They've heard it's all___ up - hill,___

D
A
D
Bm
E♭
B♭
E♭
Cm
— but all they know is how _ they feel. ___ The world says they'll nev - er make _
1.
D.S. 𝄋
2.
E7
A/C♯
A5/D
A/C♯
A5/B
A/C♯
A5/D
F7
B♭/D
B♭5/E♭
B♭/D
B♭5/C
B♭/D
B♭5/C
_ it; love says they will. ___
B/D♯
B5/E
B/D♯
B5/C♯
Verse:
B
C/E
C5/F
C/E
C5/D
C
She's eight - y - three, _ and
E/B
B
F/C
C
he's bare - ly driv - in' a car. ___

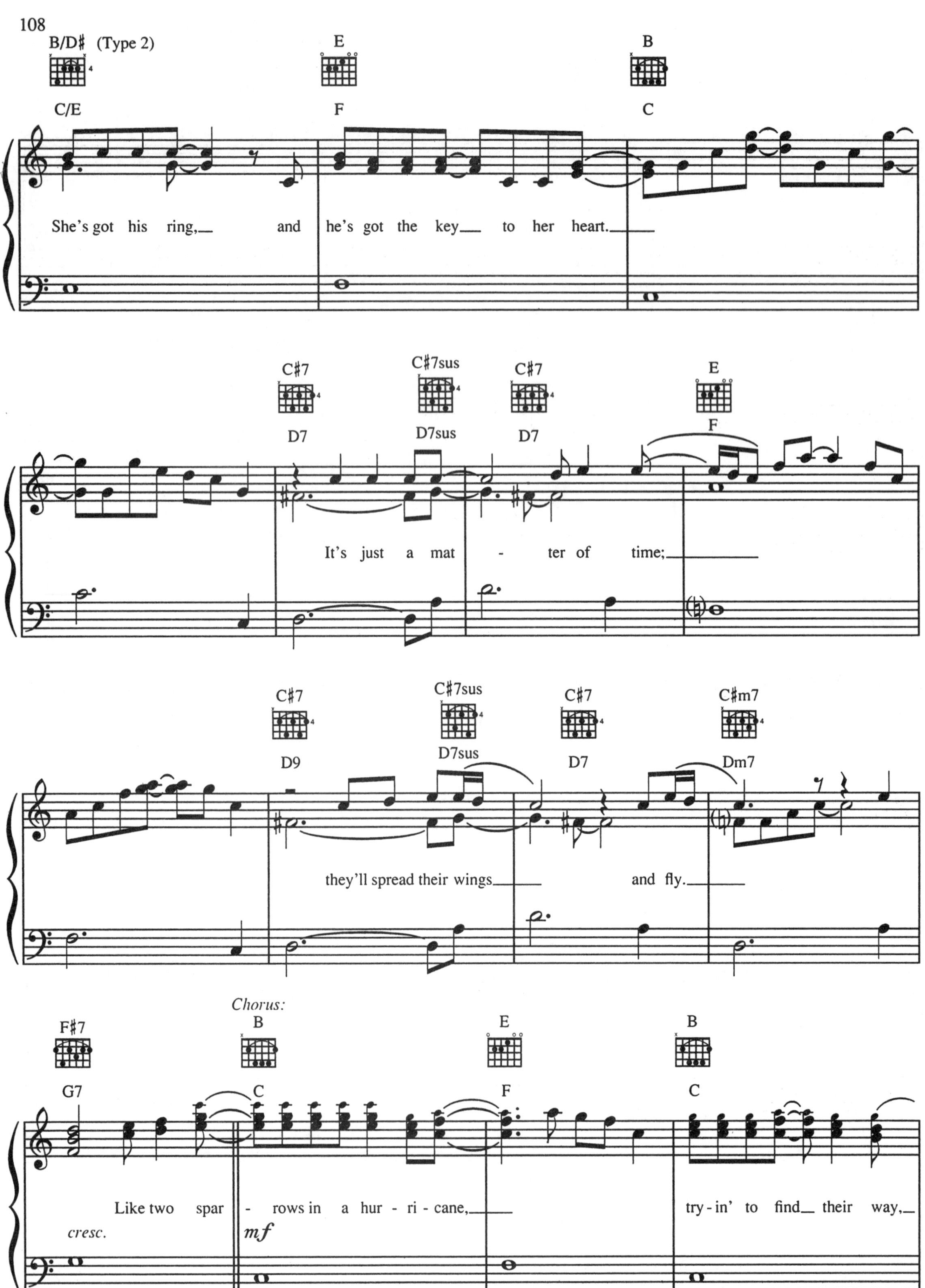
B/D♯ (Type 2)
E
B
C/E
F
C
She's got his ring, and he's got the key to her heart.
C♯7
C♯7sus
C♯7
E
D7
D7sus
D7
F
It's just a mat - ter of time;
C♯7
C♯7sus
C♯7
C♯m7
D9
D7sus
D7
Dm7
they'll spread their wings and fly.
Chorus:
F♯7
B
E
B
G7
C
F
C
Like two spar - rows in a hur - ri - cane,
try - in' to find their way,
cresc.
mf

Verse 2:
There's a baby cryin', and one more on the way.
There's a wolf at the door with a big stack of bills they can't pay.
The clouds are dark, and the wind is high,
But they can see the other side.
(To Chorus:)

STRAWBERRY WINE

Words and Music by
MATRACA BERG and GARY HARRISON

Slow country ♩. = 44
D
G
Verse:
(with pedal)
D
G
D
1. He was work - ing through col - lege
on
2. See additional lyrics
A
A7
D
my grand - pa's farm.
I was thirst - ing for knowl -
G
D
Asus
- edge
and he had a car.
A
D/F♯
G
I was caught some - where be-tween a wom - an and a child,

```
#-----------------------------------PLEASE NOTE---------------------------------#
#This file is the author's own work and represents their interpretation of the #
#song. You may only use this file for private study, scholarship, or research. #
#-------------------------------------------------------------------------------#
#

Date: Wed, 05 Mar 1997 16:08:46 -0600 (CST)
From: "Tina M. Lenz" <LENZ@uwplatt.edu>
Subject: tabs: "Strawberry Wine" by Deana Carter (revision)

Strawberry Wine
by Deana Carter
transcribed by Tina Lenz

Capo 1st fret

C                          F
He was working through college
C
On my grandpa's farm
C                         F
I was thirstin' for knowledge
C             G
And he had a car
Am
I was caught somewhere between a woman and a child
Am
One restless summer we found love growing wild

On the banks of a river on a well beaten path

Ain't funny how those memories they last like

chorus:
F           C
Strawberry wine
      G
Seventeen
              Am
The hot July moon
         F
Saw everything
                   C            G
My first taste of love whoa bittersweet
                  Am
And green on the vine
F                 C
Like strawberry wine

I still remember
When thirty was old
My biggest fear was September
When he had to go
A few cards and letters and one long distance call
We drifted away like the leaves in the fall
But year after year I come back to this place
Just to remember the taste of

Chorus

Dm
The fields have grown over now
Years since they've seen the plow
There's nothing time hasn't touched
```

Bbm
Am
Was it really him or the loss of my innocence
G F
I've been missing so much
F C
Yaaaaahhhh SOLO (play Chorus) Rep Ch.

This is my version based on the one submitted by Jason Pauken. There were a few chord changes. He had the right idea. I believe the chords are correct now.

****

"Sometimes I laugh, sometimes I cry, sometimes I do both and I don't know why...I've got a passionate heart and that's just the way things are...
You and me could give it a whirl, but I'm warning you boy...
I'm an emotional girl..."

- Terri Clark

****

Tina Lenz Lenz@uwplatt.edu http://vms.www.uwplatt.edu/~lenz

```
#----------------------------------PLEASE NOTE---------------------------------#
#This file is the author's own work and represents their interpretation of the #
#song. You may only use this file for private study, scholarship, or research. #
#------------------------------------------------------------------------------#
#
```


Date: 1/9/97; 2:49:00 PM
From: "Jason Michael Pauken" <paukenja@pilot.msu.edu>
Subject: Song

Some people wanted this song for a while so here is a version that is pretty close but not totally correct

Strawberry Wine

by Deanna Carter

Tabbed by Jason Pauken

Capo 1st fret

```
Am
He was working thru college

C                 G
On my granpa's farm

Am
I was thursten for knowledge

C               G
And he had a car

Am                    C                       G
I was caught somewhere between a woman and a child

Am                    G                     G
One restless summer we found love growing wild

Am                C                     G
On the banks of a river near a well beaten path

Am                  C                G
Ain't it funny how those memories they last

Chorus
Am               C
Like Strawberry Wine

G
Seventeen

Am
The hot july moon

C            G
Saw everything

Am      C                    G
```

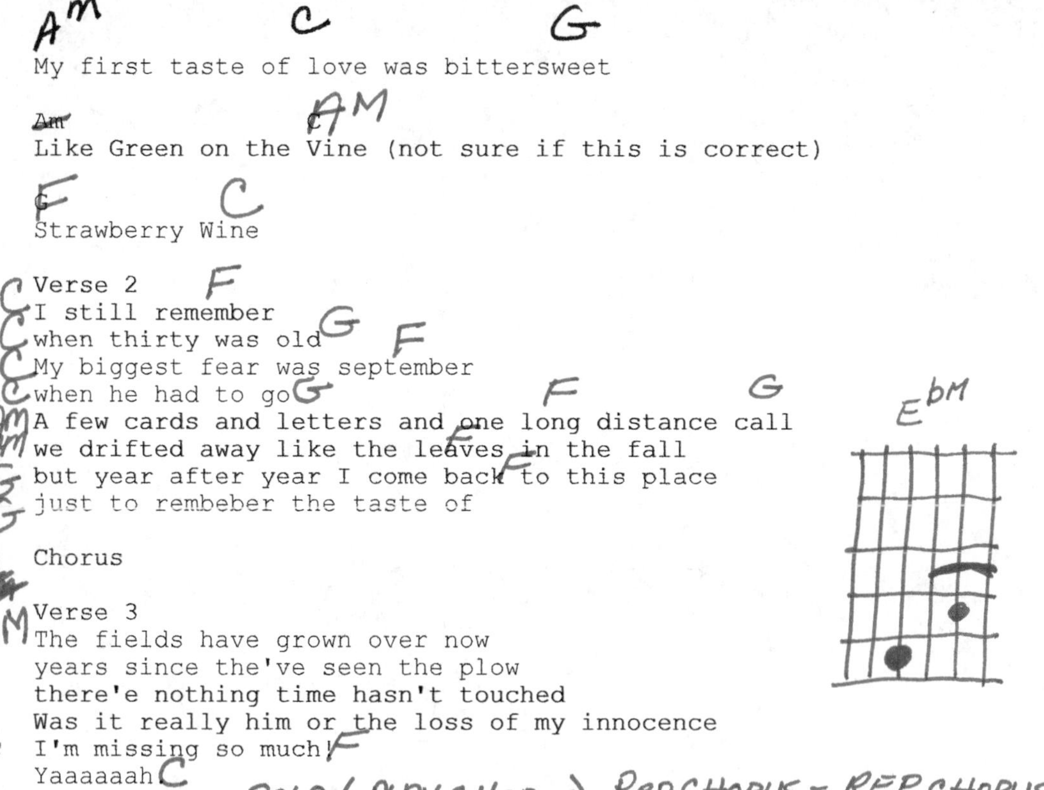

My first taste of love was bittersweet

Like Green on the Vine (not sure if this is correct)

Strawberry Wine

Verse 2
I still remember
when thirty was old
My biggest fear was september
when he had to go
A few cards and letters and one long distance call
we drifted away like the leaves in the fall
but year after year I come back to this place
just to rembeber the taste of

Chorus

Verse 3
The fields have grown over now
years since the've seen the plow
there'e nothing time hasn't touched
Was it really him or the loss of my innocence
I'm missing so much!
Yaaaaaah

That's it you should be able to pick up the strumming pattern from the cd.

Happy to give back a song since I have taken so many!

D/F♯ G A

when one rest - less sum - mer we found love grow - ing wild on the banks of the riv -

G A

- er on the well beat - en path; it's fun - ny how those mem - o - ries can last.

Chorus:

G D A/C♯

Like straw - ber - ry wine and sev - en - teen, the

Bm G

hot Ju - ly moon saw ev - ery - thing. My first taste of

D A Bm

love, whoa, bit - ter - sweet, green on the vine

G
D
1.
like straw - ber - ry wine.
G
2.
The
Bridge:
Em6
fields have grown o - ver now,
Em7
years since they've seen the plow.
Em6
There's noth-ing
Em7
time has-n't touched.
Bm
Is it real - ly him or the loss
D
of my in - no-cence
A/C♯
I've been miss - ing so much?

Verse 2:
I still remember when thirty was old,
And my biggest fear was September
When he had to go.
A few cards and letters
And one long distance call;
We drifted away like the leaves in the fall.
But year after year I come back to this place
Just to remember the taste of...
(To Chorus:)

THINKIN' ABOUT YOU

Words and Music by
TOM SHAPIRO and BOB REGAN

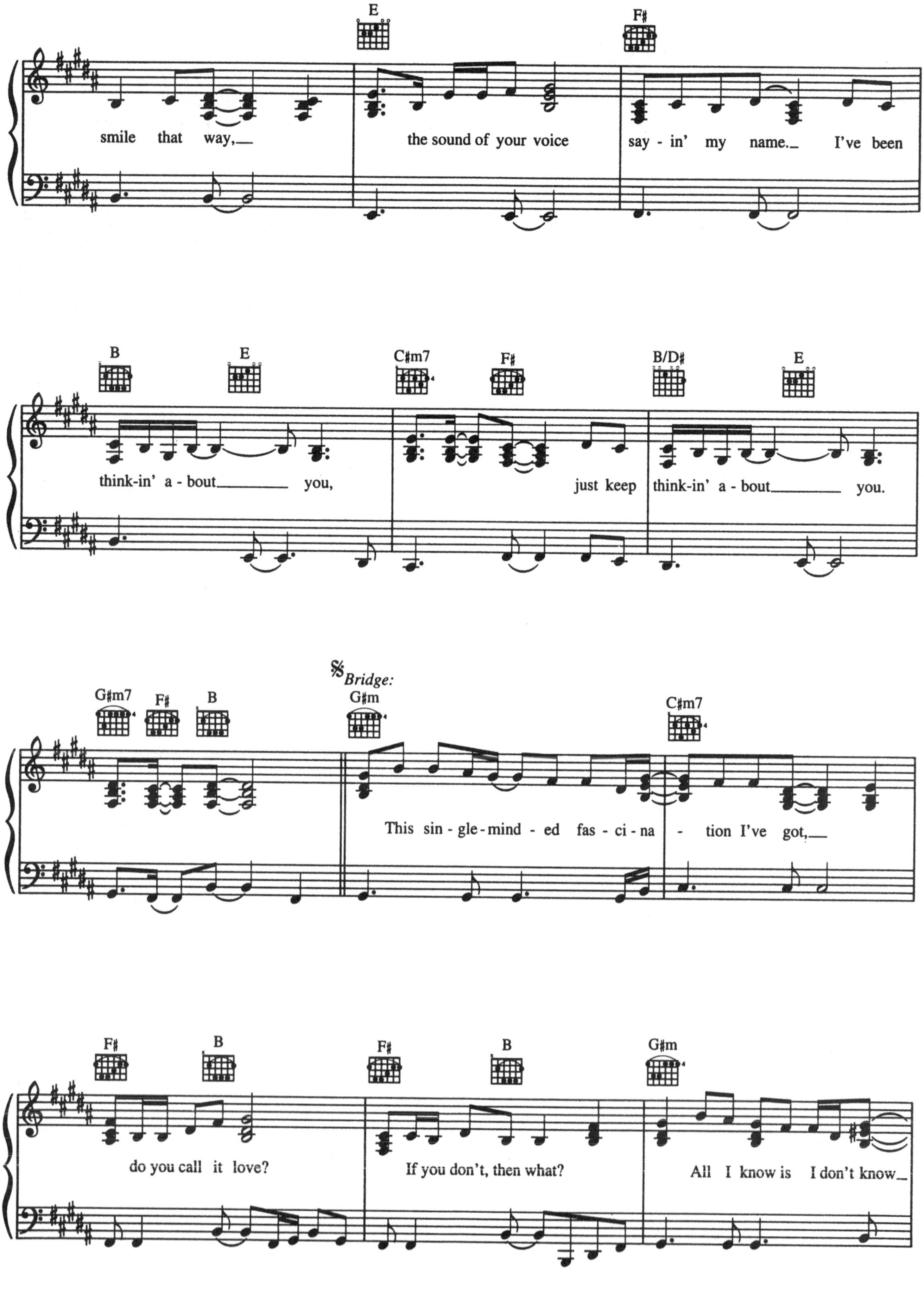

E F#

smile that way,_ the sound of your voice say - in' my name._ I've been

B E C#m7 F# B/D# E

think-in' a - bout___ you, just keep think-in' a - bout___ you.

C♯7
E
F♯
what you've done, and this train of thought ain't a-bout to jump the track that it's on.

Verses 3 & 4:
B
E
3. In the back of my mind, there's a se - cret place. But the whole world knows by the
4. See additional lyrics

F♯
B
E
smile on my face that I've been think-in' a - bout you.

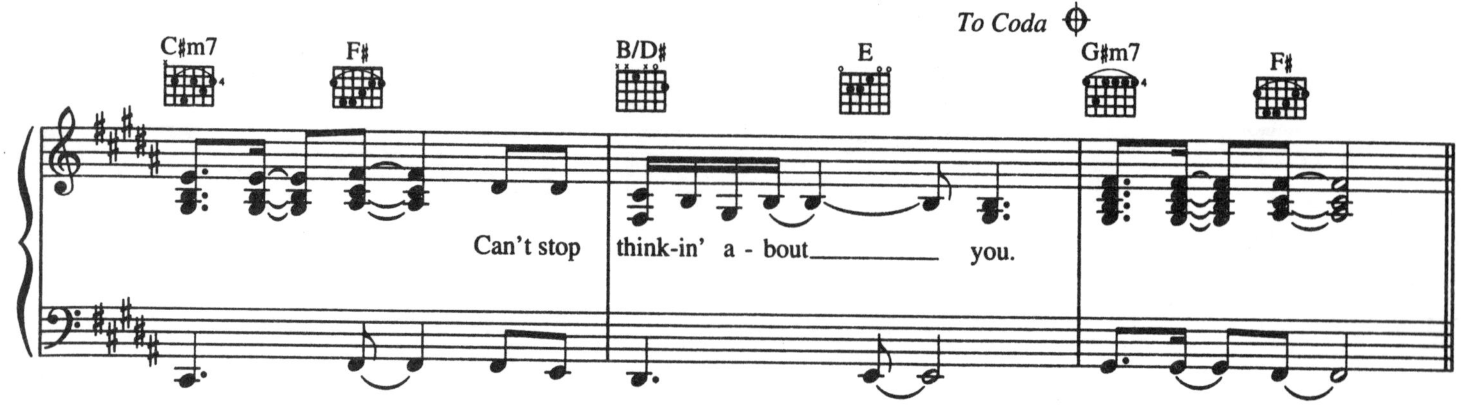
To Coda
C♯m7
F♯
B/D♯
E
G♯m7
F♯
Can't stop think-in' a - bout you.

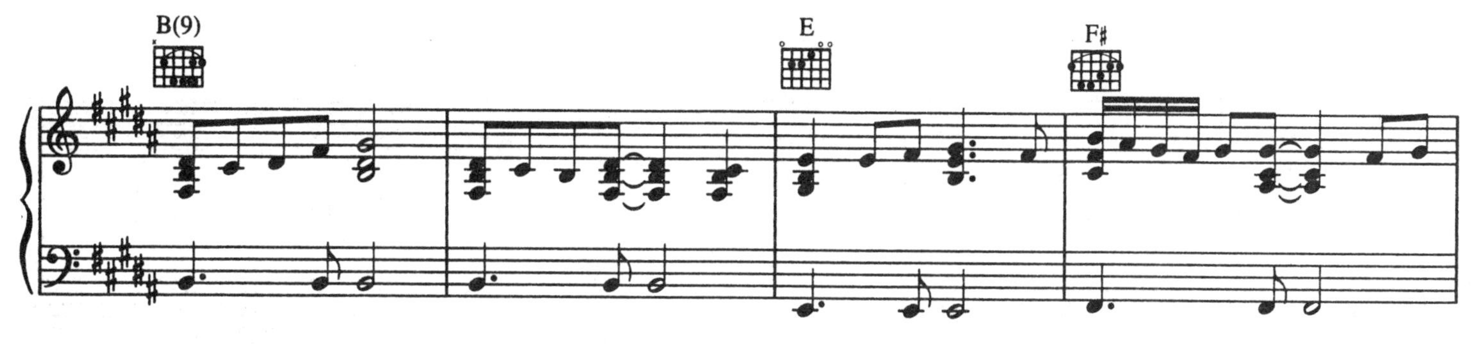

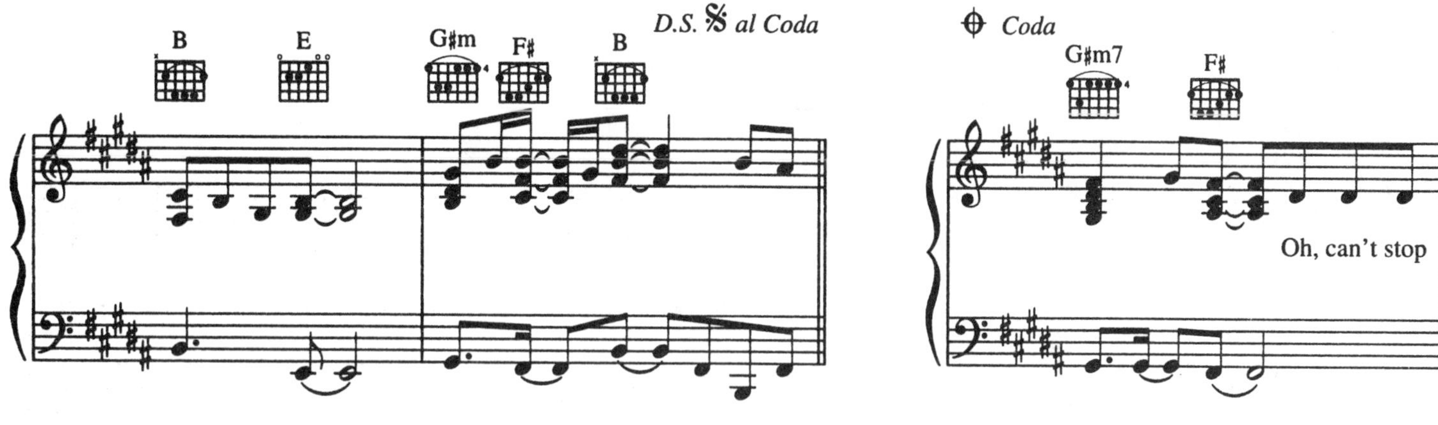

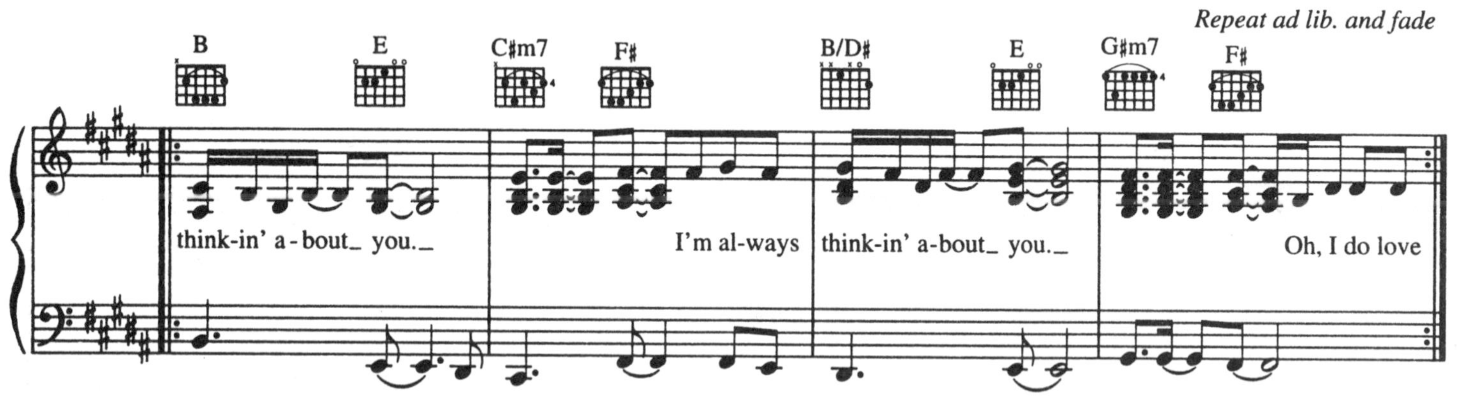

Verse 4:
I know it's crazy, callin' you this late,
When the only thing I wanted to say is that
I've been thinkin' about you,
Oh, just keep thinkin' about you.

COUNT ME IN

Words and Music by
DEANA CARTER and CHUCK JONES

Slowly ♩ = 72
F
C7sus
F
Dm
C
mf
B♭(9)
F/C
C7sus
F
Fsus
F
1. Could there
Verse:
B♭(9)
F
be a dif - f'rent end - ing to the same old sto - ry? 'Cause you're
2. See additional lyrics
B♭(9)
F/A
not the first to say you're gon - na be there for me. I need to

Dm Bb

know what's in__ your heart._____ Can you fin - ish what_ you start?_____

Gm7 C7sus C7

How can I__ be sure_ I won't_ be sor - ry? If

Chorus:

F C7sus F Bb

heart-aches and tears__ and sha - dows of doubt__ are

F C7sus Bb/D C/E

part of the deal,_ you can count me out._ But if you're

F C7sus F Dm C

talk - ing a - bout__ a game I can win,_____

Verse 2:
When you tell me you're the one I've always needed,
You don't know how much I'm wanting to believe it.
But I've heard it all before, now I'm needing something more.
A promise is no good if you can't keep it.
(To Chorus:)

YOU LIGHT UP MY LIFE

Words and Music by
JOE BROOKS

G
B♭
Cm7
B♭/D
lone in the dark, now you've come a - long.
Nev - er a - gain to be all a - lone.
And
E♭
E♭maj7
E♭7
C7
you light up my life. You give me hope
Fm
Fm7
B♭7
To Coda
to car - ry on. You light up my days and fill my
1.
E♭
B♭/D
Cm7
Fm
Fm7
B♭
nights with song.

2.
D.S. 𝄋 al Coda
E♭ B♭/D Cm7 Fm Fm7 B♭ Cm7 B♭/D
nights with song. 'Cause
Coda
G7 G7/B Cm F7 E♭/B♭
nights with song. It can't be wrong when
G7/B Cm7 F9 E♭/B♭ B♭7sus
it feels so right, 'cause you,
B♭7 A♭ E♭ B♭7 A♭(9) E♭/G Fm7 E♭
you light up my life.
rit.
a little slower

LOVE GETS ME EVERY TIME

Words and Music by
SHANIA TWAIN and R.J. LANGE

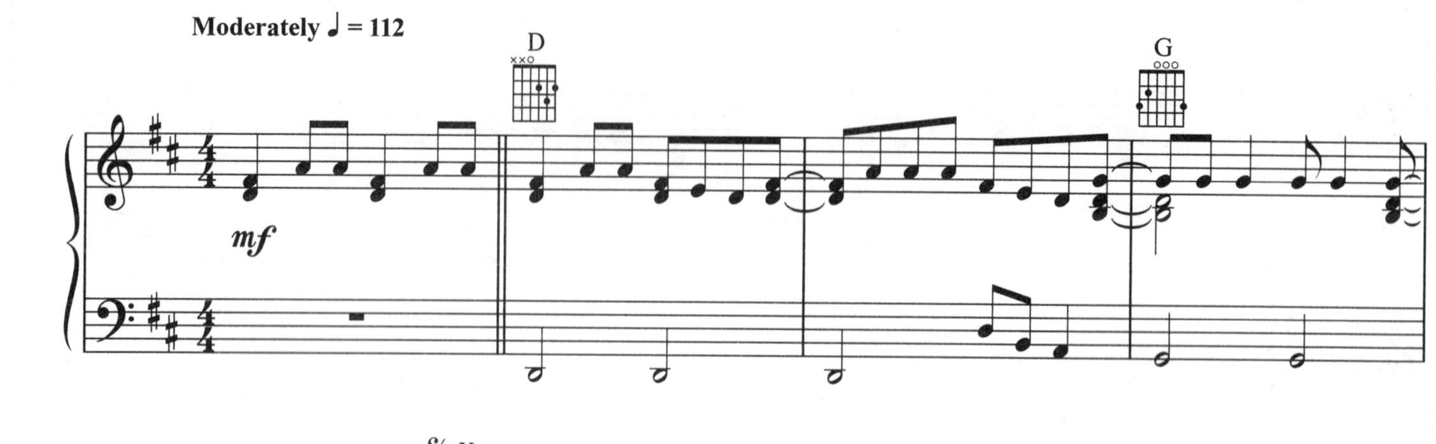
Moderately ♩ = 112
D
G
mf

Verse:
D
1. Life was go - in' great, love was gon - na have to wait, was in no
2.3. See additional lyrics

G
D
hur - ry, had no wor - ries. Stay - in' sin - gle was the plan, did - n't

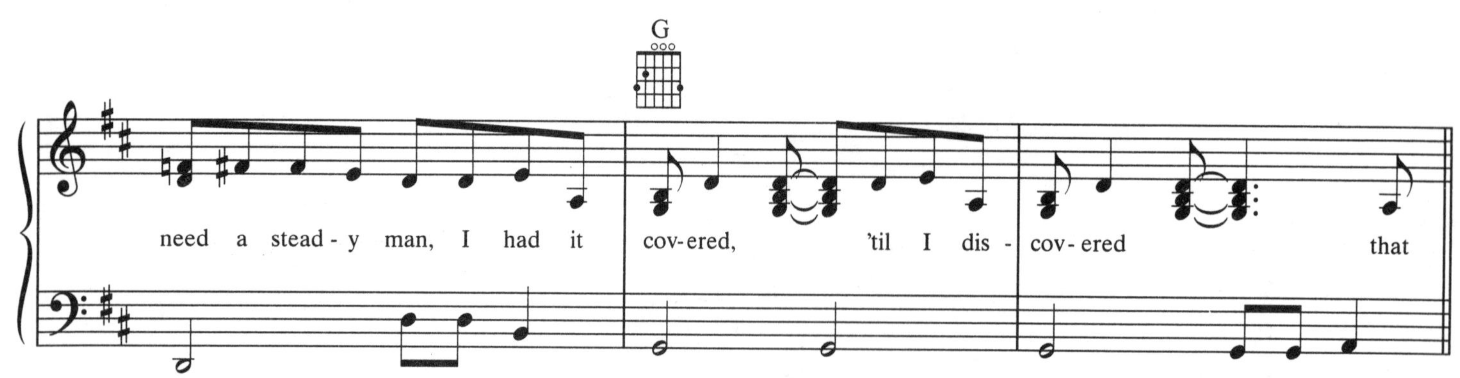
G
need a stead - y man, I had it cov - ered, 'til I dis - cov - ered that

Bridge:
Asus
G
Asus
love gets me ev - 'ry time. My heart changed my
G
N.C.
mind. And I gol' darn gone and done it. Gone and
Chorus:
G
D
done it. (Gone and done it.) I guess I fell in love. (Gone and
G
done it.) Must have been the way he walked. (Gone and done it.) Or his sweet,
D
To Coda
Asus
G
sweet talk. (Gone and done it.) I guess I

1.
N.C.
D
gol' darn gone (Gone.) and done it.
2.
D.S. 𝄋 al Coda
G
and done it.
Coda
G
done it.) It's in the way he calls my name. (Gone and done it.) And I know I'll nev - er
D
be the same. (Gone and done it.) Don't you know that
Bridge:
Asus
love gets me
G
Asus
G
ev - 'ry time. My heart changed my mind. And I

Verse 2:
I was quite content just a-payin' my own rent;
It was my place, I needed my space.
I was free to shop around, in no rush to settle down.
I had it covered, 'til I discovered...
(To Bridge:)

Verse 3:
Instrumental
(To Bridge:)

The Book of Golden Series

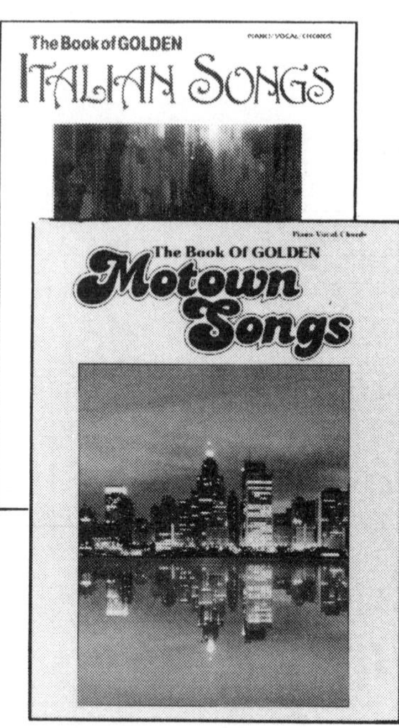

THE BOOK OF GOLDEN ALL-TIME FAVORITES
(F2939SMX) Piano/Vocal/Chords

THE BOOK OF GOLDEN BIG BAND FAVORITES
(F3172SMX) Piano/Vocal/Chords

THE BOOK OF GOLDEN BROADWAY
(F2986SMX) Piano/Vocal/Chords

THE NEW BOOK OF GOLDEN CHRISTMAS
(F2478SMB) Piano/Vocal/Chords
(F2478EOX) Easy Organ
(F2478COX) Chord Organ

THE BOOK OF GOLDEN COUNTRY MUSIC
(F2926SMA) Piano/Vocal/Chords

THE BOOK OF GOLDEN HAWAIIAN SONGS
(F3113SMX) Piano/Vocal/Chords

THE BOOK OF GOLDEN IRISH SONGS
(F3212SMX) Piano/Vocal/Chords

THE BOOK OF GOLDEN ITALIAN SONGS
(F2907SMX) Piano/Vocal/Chords

THE BOOK OF GOLDEN JAZZ
(F3012SMX) Piano/Vocal/Chords

THE NEW BOOK OF GOLDEN LATIN SONGS
(F3049SMX) Piano/Vocal/Chords

THE NEW BOOK OF GOLDEN LOVE SONGS
(F2415SOX) Organ

THE BOOK OF GOLDEN MOTOWN SONGS
(F3144SMX) Piano/Vocal/Chords

THE NEW BOOK OF GOLDEN MOVIE THEMES, Volume 1
(F2810SMX) Piano/Vocal/Chords

THE NEW BOOK OF GOLDEN MOVIE THEMES, Volume 2
(F2811SMX) Piano/Vocal/Chords

THE BOOK OF GOLDEN POPULAR FAVORITES
(F2233SMX) Piano/Vocal/Chords

THE BOOK OF GOLDEN POPULAR PIANO SOLOS
(F3193P9X) Intermediate/ Advanced Piano

THE BOOK OF GOLDEN ROCK 'N' ROLL
(F2830SMB) Piano/Vocal/Chords

THE NEW BOOK OF GOLDEN WEDDING SONGS
(F2265SMA) Piano/Vocal/Chords